IN ASSOCIATION WITH

✗ SQA

HODDER
GIBSON

Model Papers

WITH ANSWERS

PLUS: Official SQA 2014 & 2015
Past Papers With Answers

# National 5
# Computing
# Science

Model Papers, 2014 & 2015 Exams

HODDER
GIBSON
AN HACHETTE UK COMPANY

This book contains the official SQA 2014 and 2015 Exams for National 5 Computing Science, with associated SQA approved answers modified from the official marking instructions that accompany the paper.

In addition the book contains model papers, together with answers, plus study skills advice. These papers, some of which may include a limited number of previously published SQA questions, have been specially commissioned by Hodder Gibson, and have been written by experienced senior teachers and examiners in line with the new National 5 syllabus and assessment outlines, Spring 2013. This is not SQA material but has been devised to provide further practice for National 5 examinations in 2014 and beyond.

Hodder Gibson is grateful to the copyright holders, as credited on the final page of the Answer Section, for permission to use their material. Every effort has been made to trace the copyright holders and to obtain their permission for the use of copyright material. Hodder Gibson will be happy to receive information allowing us to rectify any error or omission in future editions.

Hachette UK's policy is to use papers that are natural, renewable and recyclable products and made from wood grown in sustainable forests. The logging and manufacturing processes are expected to conform to the environmental regulations of the country of origin.

Orders: please contact Bookpoint Ltd, 130 Park Drive, Milton Park, Abingdon, Oxon OX14 4SE. Telephone: (44) 01235 827720. Fax: (44) 01235 400454. Lines are open 9.00–5.00, Monday to Saturday, with a 24-hour message answering service. Visit our website at www.hoddereducation.co.uk. Hodder Gibson can be contacted direct on: Tel: 0141 848 1609; Fax: 0141 889 6315; email: hoddergibson@hodder.co.uk

This collection first published in 2015 by
Hodder Gibson, an imprint of Hodder Education,
An Hachette UK Company
2a Christie Street
Paisley PA1 1NB

Typeset by Aptara, Inc.

Printed in the UK

A catalogue record for this title is available from the British Library

ISBN: 978-1-4718-6053-9

3 2 1

2016 2015

# Introduction

## Study Skills – what you need to know to pass exams!

### Pause for thought

Many students might skip quickly through a page like this. After all, we all know how to revise. Do you really though?

### Think about this:

"IF YOU ALWAYS DO WHAT YOU ALWAYS DO, YOU WILL ALWAYS GET WHAT YOU HAVE ALWAYS GOT."

Do you like the grades you get? Do you want to do better? If you get full marks in your assessment, then that's great! Change nothing! This section is just to help you get that little bit better than you already are.

There are two main parts to the advice on offer here. The first part highlights fairly obvious things but which are also very important. The second part makes suggestions about revision that you might not have thought about but which WILL help you.

## Part 1

DOH! It's so obvious but …

### Start revising in good time

Don't leave it until the last minute – this will make you panic.

Make a revision timetable that sets out work time AND play time.

### Sleep and eat!

Obvious really, and very helpful. Avoid arguments or stressful things too – even games that wind you up. You need to be fit, awake and focused!

### Know your place!

Make sure you know exactly **WHEN and WHERE** your exams are.

### Know your enemy!

**Make sure you know what to expect in the exam.**

How is the paper structured?

How much time is there for each question?

What types of question are involved?

Which topics seem to come up time and time again?

Which topics are your strongest and which are your weakest?

Are all topics compulsory or are there choices?

### Learn by DOING!

There is no substitute for past papers and practice papers – they are simply essential! Tackling this collection of papers and answers is exactly the right thing to be doing as your exams approach.

## Part 2

People learn in different ways. Some like low light, some bright. Some like early morning, some like evening / night. Some prefer warm, some prefer cold. But everyone uses their BRAIN and the brain works when it is active. Passive learning – sitting gazing at notes – is the most INEFFICIENT way to learn anything. Below you will find tips and ideas for making your revision more effective and maybe even more enjoyable. What follows gets your brain active, and active learning works!

### Activity 1 – Stop and review

#### Step 1

When you have done no more than 5 minutes of revision reading STOP!

#### Step 2

Write a heading in your own words which sums up the topic you have been revising.

#### Step 3

Write a summary of what you have revised in no more than two sentences. Don't fool yourself by saying, "I know it, but I cannot put it into words". That just means you don't know it well enough. If you cannot write your summary, revise that section again, knowing that you must write a summary at the end of it. Many of you will have notebooks full of blue/black ink writing. Many of the pages will not be especially attractive or memorable so try to liven them up a bit with colour as you are reviewing and rewriting. **This is a great memory aid, and memory is the most important thing.**

## Activity 2 – Use technology!

Why should everything be written down? Have you thought about "mental" maps, diagrams, cartoons and colour to help you learn? And rather than write down notes, why not record your revision material?

What about having a text message revision session with friends? Keep in touch with them to find out how and what they are revising and share ideas and questions.

Why not make a video diary where you tell the camera what you are doing, what you think you have learned and what you still have to do? No one has to see or hear it, but the process of having to organise your thoughts in a formal way to explain something is a very important learning practice.

Be sure to make use of electronic files. You could begin to summarise your class notes. Your typing might be slow, but it will get faster and the typed notes will be easier to read than the scribbles in your class notes. Try to add different fonts and colours to make your work stand out. You can easily Google relevant pictures, cartoons and diagrams which you can copy and paste to make your work more attractive and **MEMORABLE**.

## Activity 3 – This is it. Do this and you will know lots!

### Step 1

In this task you must be very honest with yourself! Find the SQA syllabus for your subject (www.sqa.org.uk). Look at how it is broken down into main topics called MANDATORY knowledge. That means stuff you MUST know.

### Step 2

BEFORE you do ANY revision on this topic, write a list of everything that you already know about the subject. It might be quite a long list but you only need to write it once. It shows you all the information that is already in your long-term memory so you know what parts you do not need to revise!

### Step 3

Pick a chapter or section from your book or revision notes. Choose a fairly large section or a whole chapter to get the most out of this activity.

With a buddy, use Skype, Facetime, Twitter or any other communication you have, to play the game "If this is the answer, what is the question?". For example, if you are revising Geography and the answer you provide is "meander", your buddy would have to make up a question like "What is the word that describes a feature of a river where it flows slowly and bends often from side to side?".

Make up 10 "answers" based on the content of the chapter or section you are using. Give this to your buddy to solve while you solve theirs.

### Step 4

Construct a wordsearch of at least 10 × 10 squares. You can make it as big as you like but keep it realistic. Work together with a group of friends. Many apps allow you to make wordsearch puzzles online. The words and phrases can go in any direction and phrases can be split. Your puzzle must only contain facts linked to the topic you are revising. Your task is to find 10 bits of information to hide in your puzzle, but you must not repeat information that you used in Step 3. DO NOT show where the words are. Fill up empty squares with random letters. Remember to keep a note of where your answers are hidden but do not show your friends. When you have a complete puzzle, exchange it with a friend to solve each other's puzzle.

### Step 5

Now make up 10 questions (not "answers" this time) based on the same chapter used in the previous two tasks. Again, you must find NEW information that you have not yet used. Now it's getting hard to find that new information! Again, give your questions to a friend to answer.

### Step 6

As you have been doing the puzzles, your brain has been actively searching for new information. Now write a NEW LIST that contains only the new information you have discovered when doing the puzzles. Your new list is the one to look at repeatedly for short bursts over the next few days. Try to remember more and more of it without looking at it. After a few days, you should be able to add words from your second list to your first list as you increase the information in your long-term memory.

## FINALLY! Be inspired...

Make a list of different revision ideas and beside each one write **THINGS I HAVE** tried, **THINGS I WILL** try and **THINGS I MIGHT** try. Don't be scared of trying something new.

And remember – "FAIL TO PREPARE AND PREPARE TO FAIL!"

# National 5 Computing Science

The National 5 Computing Science exam is worth 90 marks. That is 60% of your overall mark. The remaining 40% of your overall mark (60 marks) comes from the supervised assignment which you will complete in class.

## The exam

Approximately half of the marks in the question paper will be awarded for questions related to *Software Design and Development*, and half to *Information Systems Design and Development*.

Candidates will complete the question paper in 1 hour and 30 minutes.

**Section 1** will have 20 marks and will consist of short answer questions assessing breadth of knowledge from across both Units. Most questions will have 1–2 marks.

**Section 2** will have 70 marks and will consist of approximately 6–8 extended response questions, each with approximately 8–12 marks. Questions will be of a problem-solving nature rather than direct recall and will include extended descriptions and explanations.

Questions related to Software Design and Development will cover the following areas:

- computational constructs and concepts
- explaining code
- writing code
- data types and structures
- software development — design, testing, documentation
- low level operations and computer architecture.

Questions related to programming will use the form of 'pseudocode' below:

Variable types: INTEGER, REAL, BOOLEAN, CHARACTER

Structured types: ARRAY, STRING

System entities: DISPLAY, KEYBOARD

Assignment: SET … TO …

Conditions: IF .. THEN .. (ELSE) … END IF

Conditional repetition: WHILE … DO … END WHILE

REPEAT … UNTIL …

Fixed repetition: REPEAT … TIMES … END REPEAT

Iteration: FOR .. FROM .. TO .. DO .. END FOR

FOR EACH … FROM … DO … END FOR EACH

Input/output: RECEIVE … FROM …

SEND … TO ..

Operations: -, +, *, /, ^, mod, &

Comparisons: =, ¹, <, <=, >, >=

Logical operators: AND, OR, NOT

Pre-defined functions: id (parameters)

If you are required to write in code then you can use any programming language with which you are familiar.

Questions related to Information Systems Design and Development will cover the following areas:

- database design, structures, links and operations
- website design, structures and links
- coding (including HTML and Javascript)
- media types, including file size calculations
- information system development — purpose, features, user interface, testing
- technical implementation (hardware, software, storage, networking/connectivity)
- security, legal and environmental issues.

## General advice

Remember to read the questions carefully and answer what is being asked.

### Trade names

It is never acceptable to use a company name, such as Microsoft Access or Serif Web-Plus etc. in an answer. Use the generic terms such as databases or web-design packages.

### Conversion

If you are asked to convert a number into an 8-bit binary number make sure that your answer has 8 bits!

## Technical terminology

It is important that the correct technical terminology is used e.g. USB flash drive – not USB pen, USB stick, pen drive or other commonly used expressions.

### Units

Remember, there are 1024 bytes in a Kilobyte, not 1000. There are:

- 1024 Kilobytes in a Megabyte
- 1024 Megabytes in a Gigabyte
- 1024 Gigabytes in a Terabyte.

### Data structure

The only data structure you need to know at National 5 is one-dimensional arrays.

### Memory

Many candidates confuse RAM memory with backing storage. Remember, RAM memory is used to store programs and data temporarily while the program is being used. Backing storage is used to hold programs and data permanently until you are ready to use them. When you open an application it is taken from the backing storage (e.g. hard disc drive) and placed into the RAM memory.

## Technical implementation

Use your common sense when thinking about the reasons why you would choose a particular type of hardware. Does it have to be portable? Does it require fast processing ability? What is the most sensible storage device? What is the best networking solution for this particular task?

## Calculating storage requirements

When calculating the storage requirements for photographs, too many candidates forget that DPI must be squared. Remember to multiply the number of bits required to store the colour – NOT the number of colours!

For example, an image measures 3 inches by 4 inches and has a resolution of 600dpi in 8 colours

= 3 x 4 x 600 x 600 x 3 (3 bits can give 8 combinations of colours)

= 12960000 bits = 12960000/8 =1620000 bytes

= 1620000/1024 = 1582.03 Kb = 1882.03 / 1024

= 1.54 Mb

## Storage devices

Candidates often confuse the three main types of storage devices:

- Magnetic – hard disk drives, floppy disc drives, magnetic tape (DAT)
- Solid state – USB flash drives
- Optical – CD-ROM, CD-R, CD-RW, DVD-ROM, DVD-R, DVD-RW and Blu-Ray.

## Computers and the Law

Candidates must give the correct full names of the appropriate laws such as the "Data Protection Act", "Computer Misuse Act", "Health & Safety Regulations", "Communications Act" and "Copyright, Design and Patents Act".

## Interfaces

Many candidates forget why an interface is required. Remember that an interface changes electrical voltages, changes analogue to digital, buffers data and deals with control signals.

## Pre-defined functions

Remember that pre-defined functions are built-in sections of code that have been written and tested and are available for programmers to use. They include common functions such as random numbers and rounding.

# Good luck!

Remember that the rewards for passing National 5 Computing Science are well worth it! Your pass will help you get the future you want for yourself. In the exam, be confident in your own ability. If you're not sure how to answer a question, trust your instincts and just give it a go anyway. Keep calm and don't panic! GOOD LUCK!

## NATIONAL 5

# Model Paper 1

Whilst this Model Paper has been specially commissioned by Hodder Gibson for use as practice for the National 5 exams, the key reference documents remain the SQA Specimen Paper 2013 and the SQA Past Papers 2014 and 2015.

National
Qualifications
MODEL PAPER 1

# Computing Science

Duration — 1 hour and 30 minutes

**Total marks — 90**

**SECTION 1 — 20 marks**

Attempt ALL questions in this section.

**SECTION 2 — 70 marks**

Attempt ALL questions in this section.

Read all questions carefully before attempting.

Write your answers in the spaces provided, using **blue** or **black** ink.

Show all workings.

Before leaving the examination room you must give this booklet to the Invigilator.
If you do not, you may lose all the marks for this paper.

MARKS | DO NOT WRITE IN THIS MARGIN

## SECTION 1 – 20 marks

### Attempt ALL questions

1. State how a computer system represents characters.    **1**

2. Convert the *binary* number 100001 into a *decimal* number. Show all working.    **1**

3. Explain how data is transferred from the *memory* into the *processor*.    **1**

4. Dot has received a text file from her friend Sara but is unable to access it with her text processing software. Explain how you can ensure that another computer user can access your text processing files that you have sent them.    **1**

5. Solid state storage devices are much more difficult to damage than magnetic disks. State **two** reasons why some laptop manufacturers are still using magnetic disks.    **2**

6. Explain the advantage of using *cloud storage* compared to local servers.    **1**

7. Describe what should happen to the data when you are accessing online banking?    **1**

MARKS | DO NOT WRITE IN THIS MARGIN

8.  State the *law* you are breaking when you download a film from the Internet without paying for it.      1

    _____

9.  Name a *standard design notation* that you could use to plan a solution to a problem.      1

    _____

10. Describe why *keylogging* is such a security risk.      2

    _____

    _____

11. Marion is looking at two laptops in a shop but is unsure which she should buy. State **two** criteria, which would help you decide which laptop was better than another.      2

    _____

    _____

12. The *pseudocode* below shows a selection of code to decide whether you are entitled to a school bus pass.

    ```
    Line 1. IF age>5 OR age<18 THEN
    Line 2. SEND ["Eligible for School Bus Pass"] TO DISPLAY
    Line 3. END IF
    ```

    When tested the program is found to have an error.

    Explain the error in the program.      1

    _____

    _____

13. Explain why the following code is not good practice.      1

    ```
    Line 1.      RECEIVE L FROM keyboard
    Line 2.      RECEIVE b FROM keyboard
    Line 3.      SET A TO L*B
    Line 4.      SEND[A] TO DISPLAY
    ```

    _____

    _____

MARKS

**14.** State the task you would be undertaking if you were using *HTML*?

1

_____

_____

**15.** Explain what a *hyperlink* is used for in a web page.

1

_____

_____

**16.** State the type of *construct* used in the following code.

1

```
Line 1.      REPEAT
Line 2.            RECEIVE code FROM KEYBOARD
Line 3.      UNTIL code=7741
Line 4.      DISPLAY ["Door Open"]
```

_____

_____

**17.** State the type of *error* you have if you make a spelling mistake when typing in your code.

1

_____

_____

MARKS | DO NOT WRITE IN THIS MARGIN

### SECTION 2 — 70 marks

### Attempt ALL questions

18. Michelle has to buy 20 computers to replace the old stand-alone desktop computers that her company uses at present.

    (a) Describe **two** advantages of replacing the desktop computers with tablet computers.

    2

    _____

    _____

    _____

    _____

    (b) Michelle's friend suggests that she should link the new computers using a *peer-to-peer network* rather than a *client-server network* as it's cheaper.

    Describe **two** reasons why this is not a good solution.

    2

    _____

    _____

    _____

    _____

    (c) Michelle wants the new computers to use *biometric security*.

    Describe **two** different ways in which computers can use biometric security.

    2

    _____

    _____

    _____

    _____

    (d) Describe what *data security precaution* the company must undertake with the old computers before they are decommissioned.

    1

    _____

    _____

**Question 18 (continued)**

MARKS

(e) Describe what should happen to the old equipment now that the company no longer want it.

2

_____

_____

_____

_____

**Total marks** 9

19. A program is required to display a motorway warning sign if a truck is:

- higher than 200 cm

- heavier than 2.4 tonnes.

```
Line 1     RECEIVE weight FROM sensor
Line 2     RECEIVE height  FROM sensor
Line 3     IF                              THEN
Line 4          DISPLAY["Do not proceed"]
Line 5          DISPLAY["Turn left at next junction"]
Line 6     END IF
```

(a) Complete the missing *pseudocode* for line 3.

3

_____

_____

_____

(b) Complete the table below to show what *test data* you would use to test the program.

3

| Type of test data | Test Data | |
|---|---|---|
| Normal | Height = | Weight = |
| Extreme | Height = | Weight = |
| Exceptional | Height = | Weight = |

**Question 19 (continued)**

MARKS

(c) Describe what should happen if you test the program with *negative data*.    1

_____

_____

(d) The information from the sensors is sent to the local police CCTV operators who check that the trucks turn left at the next junction.

State the most appropriate method of transmitting the *data* from the sensor to the police computer.    1

_____

_____

**Total marks   8**

20. A programming language provides the following pre-defined functions.

```
Right(d) - turns right d number of degrees
Left(d) - turns left d number of degrees
Forward(p) - Draws a line of p pixels
Move(p) - moves without drawing a line of p pixels
```

E.g. To draw a triangle our code would be:

| Pseudocode | Output |
|---|---|
| Right(30)<br>Forward(100)<br>REPEAT 2 TIMES<br>    Right(120)<br>    Forward(100)<br>END REPEAT | |

**Question 20 (continued)**

MARKS

(a) Write the *code* that would create the following output:    3

| Pseudocode | Output |
|------------|--------|
|            |        |

(b) The graphic could be saved as a *bit-mapped graphic* or a *vector graphic*.

Describe **two** advantages of saving the graphic as a vector compared to a bit-mapped.    2

_____

_____

_____

_____

(c) The graphic is saved as a bit-map image with a resolution of 400 x 400 pixels using four colours.

Calculate the storage requirements of the graphic. Give your answer in appropriate units.

Show your working.    3

_____

_____

_____

_____

(d) Name a *standard file format* that you may use to save the graphic.    1

_____

_____

**Total marks    9**

MARKS | DO NOT WRITE IN THIS MARGIN

21.  Bright Red Publishing have multiple choice tests available on the Internet like the example below.

| How many bytes are in a Kilobyte? | |
| --- | --- |
| A | 8 |
| B | 1000 |
| C | 1024 |
| D | 8192 |

The user types in the letter that corresponds to the correct answer.

(a)  Describe **two** problems that this type of interface could have.    2

_____

_____

_____

_____

(b)  Using pseudocode, or a language of your choice, write the _input validation psuedocode_ which will validate that the input is either A, B, C or D.    4

**Question 21 (continued)**

(c) Describe clearly with reference to *values* and *variables*, what the following *pseudocode* does.    3

```
Line 1.    SET wrong=0
Line 2.    SET right=0
Line 3.    RECEIVE answer FROM keyboard
Line 4.    IF answer=C THEN
Line 5.        SET correct=correct+1
Line 6.    ELSE
Line 7.        SET wrong=wrong +1
Line 8.    END IF
```

_____

_____

_____

_____

_____

_____

_____

_____

(d) While the program is being developed an *interpreter* is used rather than a *compiler*.

Explain why an *interpreter* is used rather than a *compiler* at this stage.    1

_____

_____

_____

_____

**Total marks  10**

MARKS | DO NOT WRITE IN THIS MARGIN

22. Heatcon make central heating controllers that turn on the heating when it becomes cold and turn them off when it becomes too warm.

(a) The *pseudocode* below shows how the heating is controlled.

```
Line 1          REPEAT
Line 2          RECIEVE temperature FROM sensor
Line 3          IF temperature<10 THEN
Line 4              SEND on TO boiler
Line 5          END IF
Line 6          IF temperature>20 THEN
Line 7              SEND off TO boiler
Line 8          END IF
Line 9          UNTIL switch = off
```

Describe all the events that will occur when you run the program if the sensor gives a temperature of **16.3 degrees**.     4

_____

_____

_____

_____

_____

_____

_____

_____

(b) Explain how the value for temperature is stored in the computer system.     2

_____

_____

_____

_____

**Question 22 (continued)**

MARKS | DO NOT WRITE IN THIS MARGIN

(c) State the *data type* that is used for the variable boiler in this program.    **1**

_____

_____

(d) Explain what connects the computer systems to the actual boiler and sensors to allow them to be controlled.    **1**

_____

_____

(e) Describe what the programmer should have put in the program to help with future maintenance.    **1**

_____

_____

**Total marks    9**

23.  "MegaToten" are a rock band who are going to keep a database of their fans to keep them informed of their concerts and new releases.

| ID | Name | Address | Town | E-Mail Address | New CD |
|----|------|---------|------|----------------|--------|
| 0001 | John Smith | 7 Dundee Street | Dundee | john.smith854@Hmail.co.uk | Yes |
| 0002 | Aleesha Khan | 15 Mountcastle Drive | Edinburgh | AleeshaAOK@Coldmail.com | No |
| 0003 | Ian Brown | 112 Fairfield Cres | Glasgow | Ibrown@Coldmail.com | No |
| 0004 | Peter Gabriel | 65 Lorne Ave | Glasgow | peteGabriel77@Hmail.co.uk | No |
| 0005 | Dmitri Simpson | 17 Earls Drive | Dundee | Dsimpson@dead.co.uk | Yes |
| 0006 | Sergei Simpson | 17 Earls Drive | Dundee | Ssimpson@dead.co.uk | Yes |
| 0007 | Alison Krauss | 119 Broadfoot Mains | Glasgow | AlisonK@Hmail.co.uk | No |
| 0008 | Pablo Hewitt | 82 Sea View | Elgin | Phewitt@coldmail.com | No |
| 0009 | Karen Brown | 5 Parkhead View | Newcastle | Kbrown@unique.com | Yes |
| 0010 | Bridget Hunter | 11 Traquair Park East | Montrose | BBHunter@Coldmail.com | No |

(a) State the most appropriate field type for the "New CD" field.    **1**

_____

_____

(b) State the most appropriate field type for the "E-Mail" field.    **1**

_____

_____

**Question 23 (continued)**       MARKS

  (c)  The ID field is a *primary key*. Explain the purpose of a *primary key* in a database.    **1**

_____

_____

  (d)  Explain what "MegaToten" should do before storing any personal data.    **1**

_____

_____

  (e)  Explain how you would find all the fans who had bought a CD in Dundee.    **3**

_____

_____

_____

_____

_____

_____

  (f)  State **one** limitation of storing data in a flat file database.    **1**

_____

_____

  (g)  State the type of *verification* that could be used on the field called "Address".    **1**

_____

_____

                                          **Total marks**    **9**

**24.** "CoolDesigns" have designed a website for the ScotX clothing company. **MARKS**

Here is the design of their proposed website.

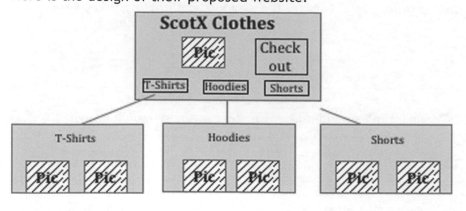

(a) State the error that "CoolDesigns" have made in the *navigation design* of the website.   **1**

_____

_____

(b) State the type of *navigation* that the website will use.   **1**

_____

_____

(c) Describe **two** tests that you would undertake on the completed website.   **2**

_____

_____

_____

_____

(d) Suggest an appropriate URL for the website.   **2**

_____

**Question 24 (continued)**

MARKS

(e) State a development in *security software* which has given confidence to customers in online purchasing.

1

_____

_____

(f) State how "ScotX" can make sure that their website is near the top of any lists produced by search engines.

1

_____

_____

(g) Code was added that allowed the graphic to be *animated* when the pointer moves over it.

State the feature of *web-authoring software* that allows code to be added to the site.

1

_____

_____

**Total marks    9**

25. This program has been designed to get each day of the week's rainfall in millimetres and give an average week's rainfall.

```
Line 1    SET Total TO 0
Line 2    FOR loop FROM 1 TO 7 DO
Line 3            RECEIVE day FROM keyboard
Line 4            RECEIVE rainfall FROM keyboard
Line 5            SET total TO total + rainfall
Line 6    END LOOP
Line 7    SET average TO average/7
Line 8    SEND ["The average weekly rainfall is ",
          average] TO DISPLAY
```

(a) Explain why "Total" is initialised to 0 at the beginning of the program.

1

_____

_____

MARKS

**Question 25 (continued)**

(b) State the type of *loop* being used in this program.        1

_____

(c) State the type of *expression* being used in line 7.        1

_____

(d) State the data types of the following variables        3

| Variable | Data type |
|----------|-----------|
| Total    |           |
| Day      |           |
| Average  |           |

(e) State what *data structure* would be required if you wanted to keep the values of the rainfall for each day.        1

_____

**Total marks  7**

**[END OF MODEL PAPER]**

# Model Paper 2

Whilst this Model Paper has been specially commissioned by Hodder Gibson for use as practice for the National 5 exams, the key reference documents remain the SQA Specimen Paper 2013 and the SQA Past Papers 2014 and 2015.

## National Qualifications
## MODEL PAPER 2

# Computing Science

Duration — 1 hour and 30 minutes

**Total marks — 90**

**SECTION 1 — 20 marks**

Attempt ALL questions in this section.

**SECTION 2 — 70 marks**

Attempt ALL questions in this section.

Read all questions carefully before attempting.

Write your answers in the spaces provided, using **blue** or **black** ink.

Show all workings.

Before leaving the examination room you must give this booklet to the Invigilator.
If you do not, you may lose all the marks for this paper.

**MARKS** | DO NOT WRITE IN THIS MARGIN

## SECTION 1 – 20 marks

### Attempt ALL questions

1. When you download music from the Internet it is in *MP3* format. Explain why some people prefer the *WAV* format that you find on a Compact Disc.    1

2. What type of *error* occurs in a program when you make a spelling mistake in the code?    1

3. Explain how the number 37.4 is stored in a computer system.    2

4. A section of HTML code is shown below.

   <b>The Kitchen Stools<u>New Album</u>

   Explain why it does not show the correct *formatting* when the code is run.    1

5. State which *bus* pinpoints the correct memory location in memory where data is to be saved?    1

6. State the purpose of a *string variable* in a computer program.    1

7. Explain why a *translator* is needed for programs written in a high level language.    1

8. Describe what you could change to allow you to store more photographs on your digital camera without increasing the capacity of the memory card.    1

MARKS | DO NOT WRITE IN THIS MARGIN

9. Mia has discovered that her next door neighbour has been accessing her wireless network.

   (a) State which *law* her neighbour has broken.    1

   _____

   (b) Describe how Mia can prevent her neighbour accessing her wireless network.    1

   _____

   _____

10. State an advantage that a *peer-to-peer network* has over a *client-server network*.    1

   _____

   _____

11. Here is part of a database used to store information on a group of family and friends.

| Forename | Surname | Address | Town | Date of Birth |
|----------|---------|---------|------|---------------|
| Sally | Thompson | 44 Dundas Street | Edinburgh | 04/05/1961 |
| Kauser | Ali | 22 Sighthill Terrace | Glasgow | 22/04/1992 |
| Denise | Shivas | 70 Queens Ave | Perth | 12/01/1999 |
| Ashima | Khan | 11 George Street | Inverness | 06/01/1975 |
| Clair | Kerr | 38 Broomhall Avenue | Kinross | 28/03/1988 |
| Joan | Sutherland | 55 St. Johns Drive | Glasgow | 28/02/1992 |
| Iain | McKenzie | 17 Home Street | Edinburgh | 03/07/1995 |
| Martin | Dailly | 24 Castle Street | Inverness | 14/09/2001 |
| Michael | Ure | 82 Echline Drive | Kirkcaldy | 24/08/1956 |
| Susan | Lamb | 14 Dundee Street | Montrose | 09/09/2001 |
| Graham | Jackson | 120 Hamilton View | Glasgow | 04/11/1992 |
| Paula | Hart | 17 Glasgow Road | Edinburgh | 16/03/1984 |

Describe what process would result in the solution being "Martin Dailly".    3

   _____

   _____

   _____

   _____

   _____

   _____

MARKS

12. The *pseudocode* below shows a program that calculates the average monthly temperature.

```
Line 1.    SET Total=0
Line 2.    FOR loop= 1 TO 30 DO
Line 3.        RECEIVE day_temperature FROM keyboard
Line 4.        SET Total = Total + day_temperature
Line 5.    END FOR
Line 6.    SET average=Total / 30
```

Explain what changes you would have to make to the program for months that have thirty-one days.

2

13. Describe the type of users who would benefit from a user interface, which had few options and large icons.

1

14. Explain, with reasons, what type of computer system would be most suited to travelling salesmen showing images of their latest products.

2

MARKS | DO NOT WRITE IN THIS MARGIN

**SECTION 2 — 70 marks**

**Attempt ALL questions**

15. Alison works for a design company and has created this image using a vector graphics package.

(a) State **two** reasons why she would not have created this image using a bit-mapped graphics package.

2

_____

_____

(b) State what standard *file type* she would use to save this file.

1

_____

(c) Alison finds a graphic on the Internet and incorporates it into her created image to create a logo for a new bike company.

1

   (i) Explain why this is *not legal*.

_____

_____

   (ii) Explain how Alison could use the graphic *legally*.

1

_____

_____

(d) Before Alison emails 200 photographs to the printing company she *compresses* the files.

   (i) Explain why the photographs require to be *compressed* before being e-mailed.

1

_____

_____

   (ii) Explain what effect compression may have on the photographs.

1

_____

_____

**Total marks    7**

**MARKS**

16. A program is used to control access to a secure area in a bank. You have **three** attempts to get the code correct before an alarm is sounded.

Here is the pseudocode for the program:

```
Line 1.        SET counter TO 1
Line 2.        REPEAT
Line 3.            RECEIVE pin FROM keypad
Line 4.            IF pin<>4714 THEN
Line 5.                SEND ["wrong number"] TO display
Line 6.            END IF
Line 7.            SET counter TO counter+1
Line 8.
Line 9.        IF pin=4715 THEN
Line 10.           SEND Open TO lock
Line 11.       ELSE
Line 12.           SEND Sound TO speakers
Line 13.       END IF
```

(a) Complete the missing *pseudocode* for line 8.    3

(b) When the program is tested with the correct code the alarm is sounded. State the *error* in the program.    1

(c) Explain why we need the *selection statement* after the loop has been completed.    2

(d) Why is a *conditional loop* used in the program rather than a *fixed loop*?    1

**Question 16 (continued)**

MARKS | DO NOT WRITE IN THIS MARGIN

(e) When the computer program is written, state **two** ways in which the program can be made readable.

2

_____

_____

_____

_____

(f) What *data type* is used by all the variables in the program?

1

_____

**Total marks   10**

17. Below is the structured diagram for a program to automatically display the cost of posting a parcel.

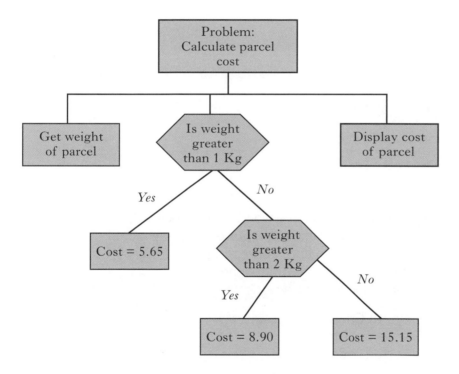

(a) Using *pseudocode*, or a programming language of your choice, write a program to implement the design above.

5

**Question 17 (continued)**

MARKS

(b) State **four** items of data that you could use to test for extreme data, assuming that the data is entered to *two decimal places*.

2

_____

_____

_____

(c) Use *pseudocode*, or a programming language of your choice, to validate the input of the weight of the parcel.

4

**Total marks  11**

18.  Ray has received the following email.

| From: | dmrkenneth@rocketmail.com |
|---|---|
| **Subject:** | Swiss Lotto Lucky Winner |
| **Attachments:** | WinnersForm.exe |
| **Message:** | Congratulations! You have won ?750,000 pounds. To claim the prize please complete the attached text file with your name, address, age, nationality, occupation, telephone no, Bank sort code and bank account no.<br><br>Mr. Kenneth Gram<br>On-line Games Director<br>Swiss Lotto London |

(a) Explain this email.

1

_____

_____

(b) Describe what could happen if you replied with the information that they ask for in the email.

1

_____

_____

_____

**Question 18 (continued)**

MARKS | DO NOT WRITE IN THIS MARGIN

(c) The attached file could contain a virus.

   (i) State a reason why you could think that the attachment is a virus.     1

   _____

   _____

   (ii) Describe **two** methods which anti-virus software use to detect viruses.     2

   _____

   _____

   _____

   _____

(d) State which *law* you are breaking by knowingly sending viruses through emails.     1

   _____

                                                    **Total marks    6**

19. Charlie has a design for his website for his music store.

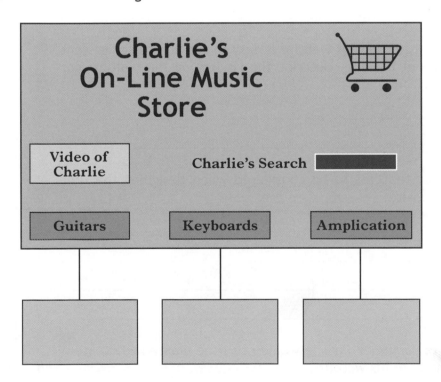

(a) What type of *links* are the "Guitars", "Keyboards" and "Amplification" navigation bars?     1

   _____

**Question 19 (continued)**                                                    MARKS

(b) Explain how Charlie's search engine differs from Google.                    1

_____

_____

(c) State the type of *addressing* that is used to link the home page to the instrument pages.                                                           1

_____

_____

(d) When Charlie tests the website, he finds that the video keeps *pausing*. State what you could do to the video to stop this problem occurring.      1

_____

_____

(e) Apart from testing that the video works, suggest **two** other tests that Charlie should make to ensure his website works correctly.                 2

_____

_____

_____

_____

(f) Charlie wants to ensure that his website is easy to use and has consistent navigation throughout the site. Describe the *navigation* that will appear on the guitar page.                                                         1

_____

_____

(g) Describe **two** other features to be considered when designing the user interface of the website.                                                   2

_____

_____

_____

_____

(h) State what type of *language* Charlie would use if he wanted to create a sign-up sheet as part of his website.                                       1

_____

_____

Total marks  10

MARKS | DO NOT WRITE IN THIS MARGIN

20. Avonvalley College keep a database of their adult students and the courses they have booked.

| Student no | Forename | Surname | Gender | Date of Birth | Class Code | Full Time |
|---|---|---|---|---|---|---|
| 153889 | Maureen | Bryce | Female | 12-12/57 | Art001 | Yes |
| 152110 | Alice | Burns | Female | 22/04/78 | Art003 | No |
| 153227 | Jasmine | Dunsmuir | Female | 13/05/67 | Art003 | No |
| 153647 | Janice | Galloway | Female | 03/06/75 | Art001 | Yes |
| 153183 | Bridget | Hunter | Female | 07/08/55 | Pho101 | Yes |
| 153856 | Jan | Pavel | Male | 19/07/72 | Com002 | No |
| 153776 | David | Perez | Male | 06/02/98 | Com002 | No |
| 153772 | Ian | Smith | Male | 01/08/58 | Pho102 | No |

(a) Describe how the database has been sorted.    2

_____

_____

(b) The database makes use of *primary keys* and *foreign keys*.

(i) Which field is the *primary key*?    1

_____

(ii) Explain what is meant by a "foreign key".    1

_____

_____

(c) What *field type* has been used in the "Full Time" field?    1

_____

(d) State **two** fields that can use *field range validation*.    2

_____

_____

(e) The College uses a website for students to book their courses.

The students can only choose their course from a list like this:

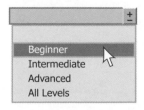

State the type of *validation* used in this situation.    1

_____

**Question 20 (continued)**

MARKS | DO NOT WRITE IN THIS MARGIN

(f) What would be the result of a search on the gender field for "Female" and the "Full Time" field for "No"?

1

(g) Describe **two** advantages of using an *electronic database* instead of a *manual database*.

2

**Total marks  11**

21. Zahera has opened up her father's laptop.

(a) She notices that the *processor* and the *RAM* memory slots are separate.

Describe how data is transferred from the *RAM* to the *processor*.

1

(b) Zahera notices that only one of the four memory slots has a *RAM chip*. Describe the benefits of adding more RAM to the laptop.

1

(c) The motherboard of the laptop comes with a number of types of *interface* such as the SATA interface for the hard disc drive.

Name and describe a purpose of an *interface* that the laptop may have.

2

**Question 21 (continued)**

(d) Zahera notices that the laptop doesn't have a *hard disc* drive but a *solid state* drive. Describe one advantage and one disadvantage of *a solid state* drive compared to a *hard disc* drive.    **2**

_____

_____

_____

_____

(e) Zahera wants a tablet computer rather than a laptop.

Describe **two** functions of a tablet that are not always available on a laptop.    **2**

_____

_____

_____

_____

**Total marks    8**

22. The following *pseudocode* has been designed to calculate the average of five test marks.

```
Line 1    RECEIVE mark1 FROM keyboard
Line 2    RECEIVE mark2 FROM keyboard
Line 3    RECEIVE mark3 FROM keyboard
Line 4    RECEIVE mark4 FROM keyboard
Line 5    RECEIVE mark5 FROM keyboard
Line 6    SET total TO mark1+mark2+mark3+mark4+mark5
Line 7    SET average TO total/5
Line 8    SEND ["The average of the five tests is ",
          average] TO DISPLAY
```

This is very inefficient code.

(a) State the most suitable *data structure* and *data type* for the variable called mark that should have been used.    **2**

_____

_____

(b) State the most suitable *data type* for the variable called total.    **1**

_____

**Question 22 (continued)**

MARKS

(c)  State the type of *construct* that should have been used in lines 1 to 5 to make a more efficient program.

1

_____

(d)  State **two** examples of *exceptional data* that you could use to test this program.

2

_____

_____

(e)  When the program is tested with *exceptional data* the programmer discovers there is a flaw to his program. What *standard algorithm* requires to be added to the program to correct this design flaw?

1

_____

_____

**Total marks**    7

**[END OF MODEL PAPER]**

# Model Paper 3

Whilst this Model Paper has been specially commissioned by Hodder Gibson for use as practice for the National 5 exams, the key reference documents remain the SQA Specimen Paper 2013 and the SQA Past Papers 2014 and 2015.

# National Qualifications
## MODEL PAPER 3

# Computing Science

Duration — 1 hour and 30 minutes

**Total marks — 90**

**SECTION 1 — 20 marks**

Attempt ALL questions in this section.

**SECTION 2 — 70 marks**

Attempt ALL questions in this section.

Read all questions carefully before attempting.

Write your answers in the spaces provided, using **blue** or **black** ink.

Show all workings.

Before leaving the examination room you must give this booklet to the Invigilator.
If you do not, you may lose all the marks for this paper.

**MARKS**

## SECTION 1 – 20 marks

### Attempt ALL questions

1. *Repetitive Strain Injury (RSI)* is one way in which using a computer can be bad for your health. Describe one way you can prevent *RSI*.    **1**

   _____

   _____

2. Many publications on the Internet are published as *PDF* files. What advantage do *PDF* files have over other formats?    **1**

   _____

   _____

3. In order to make code readable programmers should include internal commentary in their code. Describe two other methods of making code more readable.    **2**

   _____

   _____

   _____

   _____

4. Mary has decided to upgrade her digital camera from a *4 Megapixel* to a *12 Megapixel*. State one advantage and one disadvantage that her new photographs will have over her old photographs.    **2**

   _____

   _____

   _____

   _____

5. The following code creates a random number between 1 and 100.

   ```
   Let number=INT(100*RND)+1
   ```

   RND produces a random number between 0 and 1

   INT rounds to the nearest integer

   _____

   State the type of *constructs* that RND and INT belong to.    **2**

   _____

   _____

MARKS

6.  When Alice is buying a new computer she notices that she has *USB3* and *USB2* *interfaces*. Explain the advantage of *USB3* over *USB2 interfaces*.    **1**

_____

_____

7.  Many people say that the *carbon footprint* of computers is too great. Explain how computers could reduce the use of energy in other areas.    **1**

_____

_____

8.  A computer program is created to keep data about the temperature in towns around Scotland. The data is input through a very sensitive sensor, which gives the temperature to 5 decimal places.

    (a)  What type of *program construct* would you use to ensure that the data was restricted to two decimal places?    **1**

    _____

    _____

    (b)  State the *data type* that you should use to store the value of the temperature.    **1**

    _____

9.  *ROM*, *RAM* and *Registers* all store information. Explain why *ROM* is different from *RAM* and *Registers* in the way it stores information.    **1**

_____

_____

10. *Javascript* is used to add interactivity to webpages and make them more dynamic.

    Describe **two** occasions when you would use *javascript* in a webpage.    **2**

    _____

    _____

    _____

    _____

11. Describe a situation when you would decide that a *flat file structure* is not appropriate for a *database* and that *linked tables* should be used.    **1**

_____

_____

MARKS

12. Peter has moved into a flat and has discovered that he can access the Internet using his next-door neighbour's wi-fi. State two reasons why he has decided to get his own wired access to the Internet.

2

_____

_____

_____

_____

13. State the most suitable *data structure* and *data type* required for storing 100 test marks in a computer program.

2

_____

_____

MARKS | DO NOT WRITE IN THIS MARGIN

### SECTION 2 — 70 marks

### Attempt ALL questions

14. "Nile online" are designing the information form that they require their customers to complete when buying goods online.

| Field Name | | Field size | Field Type |
|---|---|---|---|
| Forename | | 25 | |
| Surname | | 25 | |
| Address | | 25 | |
| Town | | 25 | |
| Type of Credit card | | | |
| | Visa | 1 | |
| | Mastercard | 1 | |
| | Amex | 1 | |
| Credit Card Number | | 16 | |
| Expiry Date | | 8 | |
| Card Security Code | | 3 | |

(a) Complete the *field types* above for the information form.　2

(b) Describe how a *presence check* could be used to validate the data.　2

_____

_____

_____

_____

(c) State **two** fields, which could use a *length check*.　2

_____

_____

(d) Explain which of the fields would be a suitable *primary key*.　1

_____

_____

Total marks　7

**15.** Invictus games are developing a simple paddle game for a smartphone app.

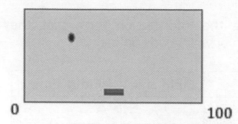

0                                                        100

The game is to be controlled in the following manner:

Press Letter Z to go left

Press letter M to move right

Press letter T to stop the game.

```
Line 1      SET x=50
Line 2      REPEAT
Line 3          RECEIVE letter FROM keyboard
Line 4          IF letter="Z" AND x>0 THEN
Line 5              SET x=x-1
Line 6          END IF
Line 7
Line 8
Line 9          END IF
Line 10         SEND paddle (x,10) TO display
Line 11     UNTIL letter ="T"
```

(a) Using *pseudocode*, or a language of your choice, complete the missing *pseudocode* to control the M key for lines 7 and 8.

4

MARKS | DO NOT WRITE IN THIS MARGIN

**Question 15 (continued)**

(b) Explain what happens when the program is tested with a letter other than Z, M or T.                    1

_____

_____

(c) State what *data type* is the variable called letter?                    1

_____

(d) Ten points are scored if the ball touches the wall behind the paddle.

Using *pseudocode*, or a language of your choice, write the line of code that increases the score.                    2

_____

_____

(e) State what *hardware information* the programmers would require to ensure that their app will work on smartphones.                    1

_____

_____

**Total marks    9**

16. The following *pseudocode* has been written to find the team with the most points.

```
Line 1    SET teams TO [Edinburgh, London, Berlin, Paris]
Line 2    SET points TO [47,27,51,51]
Line 3    SET highest TO 1
Line 4    FOR position FROM 2 TO 4
Line 5            IF points[highest]<points[position] THEN
Line 6                    SET highest TO position
Line 7            END IF
Line 8    END FOR
Line 9    SEND["The winning team is "]team[highest] TO
          display
```

(a) State the *output* from the above *pseudocode*.                    1

_____

*Page seven*

MARKS | DO NOT WRITE IN THIS MARGIN

**Question 16 (continued)**

(b) Describe the *logic error* that this program has.

1

_____

_____

(c) The first time the program was coded and run, line 7 had a *syntax error*. What could have been the problem?

1

_____

_____

(d) State the most suitable *data structure* and *data type* for the variable team.

2

_____

_____

(e) Describe what changes you would be required to make to the *pseudocode* to find the team with the lowest score.

3

_____

_____

_____

_____

_____

_____

(f) Describe what changes you would be required to make to the pseudocode if there were eight teams rather than four.

3

_____

_____

_____

_____

_____

_____

**Total marks  11**

MARKS | DO NOT WRITE IN THIS MARGIN

**17.** The "GroundNews" news agency have designed their new website.

| | |
|---|---|
| WWW.GroundNews.org.uk | **Search** |
| UK | |
| Europe | |
| Africa | **Latest** |
| Asia | |
| America | **UFO spotted over Glasgow** |

(a) What is the news agency's *URL*?   1

_____

(b) State the name of the first page of a website.   1

_____

(c) Describe what happens when you click on the internal *hyperlink* called "Africa".   1

_____

_____

(d) Describe why the search page will be limited.   1

_____

_____

(e) State a suitable *standard file format* for the video clips.   1

_____

(f) Comment on why this design would be suitable for use on a smartphone.   2

_____

_____

MARKS | DO NOT WRITE IN THIS MARGIN

**Question 17 (continued)**

(g) Describe **two** hardware limitations you should consider when designing websites for smartphones.

2

_____

_____

_____

_____

(h) The news agency will take stories sent to them from members of the public. What must the agency do to ensure they don't break the *Copyright, Designs and Patents Act*?

1

_____

_____

(i) Describe **three** tests that the news agency should undertake on their completed website.

3

_____

_____

_____

_____

_____

_____

**Total marks  13**

18.  The following is a price list for concerts depending on age.

   • Under 18 – £5

   • Between 18 and 26 – £10

   • Over 27 – £20

MARKS | DO NOT WRITE IN THIS MARGIN

**Question 18 (continued)**

(a) Using *pseudocode*, or a programming language of your choice, write a short program to output the correct ticket cost depending on the users age.    **4**

(b) State the *data type* that you would use for the variable age.    **1**

_____

(c) State the *data* that you would use to check for *extreme data* in this program.    **2**

_____

_____

(d) When the program is being developed it is run using an *interpreter*. State an advantage of using an *interpreter* rather than a *compiler* at the development of a program.    **1**

_____

_____

(e) When the program has completed testing a compiled version is made. State **two** advantages of a compiled version compared to an interpreted version.    **2**

_____

_____

MARKS

**Question 18 (continued)**

(f) Explain the difference between the *high-level language code* you have created and the compiled version.

1

_____

_____

**Total marks 11**

19. "Y3" are recording their latest music album using sound editing software on a laptop computer.

(a) The band want to buy an *external hard drive* to backup their songs.

State **two** criteria that they should use when deciding which external hard drive to buy.

2

_____

_____

(b) The music files are stored in *WAV format*, which are too large to email to their American producer. Explain how they could reduce the size of the files.

1

_____

_____

(c) Explain the advantage of saving their music files to a *cloud network*.

1

_____

_____

(d) The band are concerned that keeping their files in a *cloud network* will not be secure. Describe **two** ways in which the company running the cloud network can keep access to your files secure.

2

_____

_____

_____

_____

**MARKS**

**Question 19 (continued)**

(e) The band have downloaded a photograph for the front cover.

(i) Explain how the photograph is stored in the computer's *memory*.    2

_____

_____

_____

_____

(ii) The photograph is *1200 dpi* in four colours. Calculate the *storage requirements* of this graphic. Give your answer in appropriate units. Show your working.    3

_____

_____

_____

_____

_____

_____

**Total marks  11**

20. "Dirtcheap Flights" have an online database of all the seats that they have sold.

| Surname | Initial | E-mail address | Ref No | Flight No | From | To | Date |
|---------|---------|----------------|--------|-----------|------|-----|------|
| Brown | A | rsimpson@greenet.com | 43271 | DH006 | EDI | PRA | 17015 |
| Green | M | mgreen265@bigmail.com | 43268 | DH006 | EDI | PRA | 17015 |
| Johns | C | cjohns@ceapnet.com | 43270 | DH006 | EDI | PRA | 17015 |
| Khan | S | saheerakhan@bluenet.com | 43269 | DH006 | EDI | PRA | 17015 |
| Needy | G | mgreen265@bigmail.com | 43272 | DH006 | EDI | PRA | 17015 |
| Simpson | R | rsimpson@greenet.com | 43267 | DH006 | EDI | PRA | 17015 |
| Taylor | R | mgreen265@bigmail.com | 43273 | DH006 | EDI | PRA | 17015 |
| Cray | O | Crayclan@bluenet.com | 43277 | DH013 | LHW | AMS | 17015 |
| Fallon | D | Crayclan@bluenet.com | 43278 | DH013 | LHW | AMS | 17015 |
| Hunter | W | whunter@smalltalk.com | 43274 | DH013 | LHW | AMS | 17015 |
| McDonald | A | andymac@bluetalk.com | 43276 | DH013 | LHW | AMS | 17015 |
| Summer | Y | whunter@smalltalk.com | 43276 | DH013 | LHW | AMS | 17015 |

(a) Describe how the data has been sorted.    2

_____

_____

_____

MARKS | DO NOT WRITE IN THIS MARGIN

**Question 20 (continued)**

(b) Describe why a *relational database* is required rather than a *flat-file database*.　　**1**

_____

_____

(c) The database keeps crashing due to a large number of *pings* sent to the database server.

State what type of *network security* threat is being undertaken.　　**1**

_____

_____

(d) "Dirtcheap" are criticised in the press for having a complicated *user interface design*. Describe **two** requirements of good *interface design*.　　**2**

_____

_____

_____

_____

(e) The server that runs the database has many *interfaces* for connecting to a variety of peripherals. Describe **two** reasons why *interfaces* are required.　　**2**

_____

_____

_____

_____

**Total marks**    **8**

[END OF MODEL PAPER]

NATIONAL 5

2014

# N5

National
Qualifications
2014

Mark

## X716/75/01

# Computing Science

FRIDAY, 23 MAY

9:00 AM—10:30 AM

---

**Fill in these boxes and read what is printed below.**

Full name of centre

Town

Forename(s)

Surname

Number of seat

Date of birth

Day     Month     Year

D D   M M   Y Y

Scottish candidate number

**Total marks—90**

**SECTION 1—20 marks**

Attempt ALL questions in this section.

**SECTION 2—70 marks**

Attempt ALL questions in this section.

Write your answers clearly in the spaces provided in this booklet. Additional space for answers is provided at the end of this booklet. If you use this space you must clearly identify the question number you are attempting.

Use **blue** or **black** ink.

Show all working.

Before leaving the examination room you must give this booklet to the Invigilator; if you do not, you may lose all the marks for this paper.

SQA

**MARKS** | DO NOT WRITE IN THIS MARGIN

**SECTION 1 — 20 marks**

**Attempt ALL questions**

1. A web page can use internal and external hyperlinks.

   Explain the difference between an internal hyperlink and external hyperlink.    **2**

   _____

   _____

   _____

2. Gillian is viewing a website on her laptop.  Name the software on Gillian's laptop that enables her to do this.    **1**

   _____

3. Calculate the backing storage required for an 8 bit colour image 400 pixels by 600 pixels.

   Express your answer in Kilobytes.    **3**

4. Name the part of the processor that deals with comparisons.    **1**

   _____

**MARKS**

DO NOT WRITE IN THIS MARGIN

5. Convert the decimal value 47 into the equivalent 8-bit binary number.

1

6. State **one** problem associated with storing data in a flat file database.

1

_____

7. A bank employee has lost a laptop storing customers' personal details.

   Identify **one** *security precaution* the bank should have in place to prevent unauthorised access to this information.

1

_____

_____

8. When ordering pizza online, users select their choice from the following drop down menu:

| PIZZA ▽ |
| --- |
| Margherita |
| Hawaiian |
| Pepperoni |

State **one** advantage of this type of user interface.

1

_____

_____

[Turn over

**MARKS**

9. Before going live with a new website, the developer makes sure it matches the original design. Describe **one** other type of testing that the developer should carry out.

1

_____

_____

10. Businesses and individuals are now making use of *cloud* services instead of local storage for storing their data.

State **one** benefit of using cloud based storage instead of local storage.

1

_____

_____

11. Hussain is a technician for a new company and has been asked to prepare a presentation on networks. State **one** difference between peer-to-peer and client/server networks that he could include in his presentation.

2

| Client/Server | Peer-to-Peer |
|---|---|
|  |  |

**MARKS**

12. This pseudocode allows a user to enter the level they wish to start playing a game.

| |
|---|
| Line 1  RECEIVE level FROM (INTEGER) KEYBOARD |
| Line 2  WHILE level < 1 OR level > 10 DO |
| Line 3                    SEND "error : please re–enter level" TO DISPLAY |
| Line 4                    RECEIVE level FROM (INTEGER) KEYBOARD |
| Line 5  END WHILE |

Explain what happens if a user enters 12.                                          2

_____

_____


13. A programmer is developing a stock control program.  If a user enters a stock code number from 1 to 900, it will display the number of items in stock.

Give **one** example of _exceptional test data_ the programmer could use to test the program.                                                                              1

_____


[Turn over

MARKS | DO NOT WRITE IN THIS MARGIN

**14.** Employees can only access their company network if they enter a correct username and password. A validation program is being developed and will run each time an employee logs on.

An extract of pseudocode from the program is shown below.

```
Line 1  RECEIVE userName FROM (STRING) KEYBOARD
Line 2  RECEIVE pinNumber FROM (STRING) KEYBOARD
Line 3  IF userName VALID OR pinNumber VALID THEN
Line 4          Allow access to network
Line 5  ELSE
Line 6          SEND "Access Denied" TO SCREEN
Line 7  END IF
```

An error is noticed when the program is tested.

(a) Identify the line containing a logic error. **1**

Line ____________________

(b) State how this error should be corrected. **1**

____________________

____________________

[Turn over for Question 15 on *Page eight*

**DO NOT WRITE ON THIS PAGE**

## SECTION 2 — 70 marks

### Attempt ALL questions

15. Holibobs sells holidays to its online customers. A page from Holibobs website is shown below.

(a) State the URL of this web page.    1

MARKS | DO NOT WRITE IN THIS MARGIN

## 15. (continued)

(b)  The webpage is created using HTML and Javascript.

(i)  State the feature of HTML code that allows the webpage to be formatted.  **1**

_____

(ii)  Clicking on the "Location Map" button opens the PlanetEarth Maps website in a new window.

Explain why the HTML code for this link uses absolute addressing.  **1**

_____

_____

(iii)  The "weather widget" showing the current weather uses Javascript code.

Suggest **one** other use of Javascript that could be added to this webpage.  **1**

_____

_____

(c)  The Holibobs website includes a variety of media types which are stored using several standard file formats.

Complete the table below, indicating where the following file formats have been used on the website.

The first one has been done for you.  **2**

| File format | Example |
|---|---|
| pdf | brochure |
| mp4 | |
| jpeg | |

[Turn over

MARKS | DO NOT WRITE IN THIS MARGIN

**15. (continued)**

(d) The photo gallery features a wide range of holiday images. A photograph is going to be added to the photo gallery.

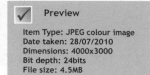

**Beach v1**

Item Type: JPEG colour image
Date taken: 28/07/2010
Dimensions: 4000x3000
Bit depth: 24bits
File size: 4.5MB

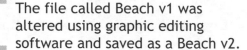

The file called Beach v1 was altered using graphic editing software and saved as a Beach v2.

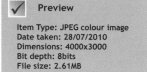

**Beach v2**

Item Type: JPEG colour image
Date taken: 28/07/2010
Dimensions: 4000x3000
Bit depth: 8bits
File size: 2.61MB

Explain why Beach v2 is being added to the photo gallery instead of Beach v1.

2

_____

_____

_____

## 15. (continued)

(e) A search is carried out for holidays in Greece leaving from "Any London" airport after 1st May 2015.

Here are some of the matching holidays.

| From | Resort | Departs | Price per person |
|------|--------|---------|------------------|
| Gatwick | Kefalonia | 19/05/2015 | £350·00 |
| Gatwick | Corfu | 30/05/2015 | £325·00 |
| Gatwick | Santorini | 07/06/2015 | £295·00 |
| Luton | Zante | 04/06/2015 | £295·00 |
| Stansted | Corfu | 04/06/2015 | £289·00 |
| Stansted | Kefalonia | 21/05/2015 | £289·00 |
| Gatwick | Kos | 19/05/2015 | £289·00 |
| Luton | Halkidiki | 03/06/2015 | £250·00 |
| Luton | Corfu | 17/05/2015 | £225·00 |
| Stansted | Zante | 28/05/2015 | £225·00 |
| Gatwick | Kos | 12/06/2015 | £199·00 |

Describe how the list is sorted. 　　　　2

_____

_____

_____

**Total marks　10**

**[Turn over**

**MARKS**

16. Jack has been asked to design a program to calculate the potential profit in a soft drink business. The program will store the costs involved in producing and selling one litre of each drink.

    The following calculations will be used to output the profit made for each litre of drink.

    **Manufacturing Cost = Water Cost + Flavouring Cost + Labour Cost**

    **Profit = Selling Price − Manufacturing Cost**

    (a) State the number of variables Jack would require in his program.

    **1**

    _____

    (b) Using pseudocode or a programming language of your choice, write a program to enter the required data, then calculate and display the profit for the soft drink business.

    **5**

    | Pseudocode | ☐ | OR | Programming Language | |
    |---|---|---|---|---|

MARKS | DO NOT WRITE IN THIS MARGIN

**16. (continued)**

(c) Jack adapts the program to ensure that **water cost** can only be entered as always greater than or equal to £0·10 and less than or equal to £0·50 per litre.

(i) State the standard algorithm that is used to ensure that data entered is acceptable.

1

_____

(ii) Complete the table below to show four different examples of test data for **water cost** and the type of each example.

3

| Test Data | Type of Test Data |
|-----------|-------------------|
| 0·05 | |
| 0·45 | normal |
| 0·10 | |
| | extreme |

**Total marks 10**

**[Turn over**

**MARKS** | DO NOT WRITE IN THIS MARGIN

17. A supermarket website is used successfully by customers using desktop computers to order groceries online.

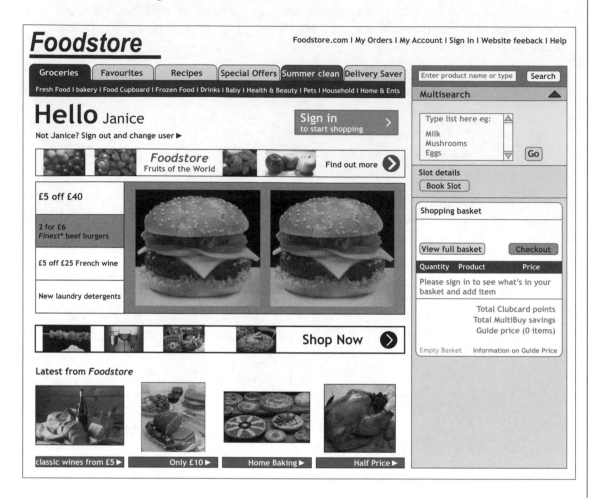

(a) The company has received complaints from some customers that the website is difficult to use on their tablet or smartphone.

Identify **two** reasons why the webpage above would be unsuitable for such portable devices.

2

Reason 1

_____

Reason 2

_____

(b) When buying items online, encryption is used. Explain why customers should be reassured by this feature.

1

_____

_____

MARKS | DO NOT WRITE IN THIS MARGIN

**17. (continued)**

(c) The supermarket is now developing a mobile application (app) for use on smartphones.

Explain why different types of smartphone would require different versions of the app.

1

_____

_____

(d) The mobile app contains a search page so that customers can find the items they want to buy from the supermarket.

Identify **two** smartphone input devices that would allow users to make use of the search features of this app.

2

_____

_____

[Turn over

**MARKS**

**17. (continued)**

(e) As well as having the mobile app and website the company provides a DVD of recipes.

Complete the table below to show which type of storage (magnetic, optical or solid state) is most appropriate for each of the following uses and why.

3

| | Type of storage | Reason |
|---|---|---|
| **Smartphone storing the app** | | |
| **Web server storing the website** | | |
| **Collection of video recipes stored on DVD** | | |

(f) The minimum amount of RAM required to run the app is 1 Gigabyte.

State what RAM stands for.

1

_____

_____

**Total marks  10**

[Turn over for Question 18 on *Page eighteen*

**DO NOT WRITE ON THIS PAGE**

MARKS | DO NOT WRITE IN THIS MARGIN

**18.** An athlete is developing a mobile application (app).

The app will allow athletes to track weight in Kg.

Part of the pseudocode for this app is shown below.

```
......
.....
Line 15    SEND "Enter your new weight" TO DISPLAY
Line 16    RECEIVE newWeight FROM (REAL) KEYBOARD
Line 17        IF newWeight > previousWeight [counter] THEN
Line 18            SEND ["You have gained weight"] TO DISPLAY
Line 19        END IF
Line 20    SET previousWeight [counter] TO newWeight
....
.....
```

(a)  (i)  Identify the line that includes a condition.                              1

Line _____

(ii)  Identify the line that stores a value in an array.                         1

Line _____

(iii)  Identify the line that accepts input values into the program.             1

Line _____

(b)  When the code for the program is written the programmer mis-types the word UNTIL, typing UNTOL instead.

State the type of programming error being described above.                       1

_____

MARKS | DO NOT WRITE IN THIS MARGIN

**18. (continued)**

(c) The pseudocode is edited to ensure that the new weight being entered is acceptable.

> ....
>
> Line 16    REPEAT
>
> Line 17            RECEIVE newWeight FROM (REAL) KEYBOARD
>
> Line 18    UNTIL newWeight > 20 AND newWeight < 70
>
> ......

(i) State the **type** of loop shown above.                                    1

_____

(ii) State an input **the user** could enter to enable the program to continue from line 18.                                    1

_____

(d) State another design notation that could have been used to design the app.                                    1

_____

(e) While the program is being implemented, the programmer stops occasionally to run the program.

State the type of translator you would recommend the programmer uses in this situation.

Explain your answer.                                    2

Translator _____

Explanation _____

_____

_____

_____

(f) State the component required to convert the data from the mobile devices touchscreen into data that can be used by the app.                                    1

_____

**Total marks  10**

MARKS | DO NOT WRITE IN THIS MARGIN

19. Ally has designed a website that encourages children to learn about energy saving and conservation.

Ally plans to include 2 sections – a personal carbon footprint calculator and a game to play.

(a) The carbon footprint calculator takes the user through a list of questions about their current energy usage.

Here are Ally's designs for some of the questions.

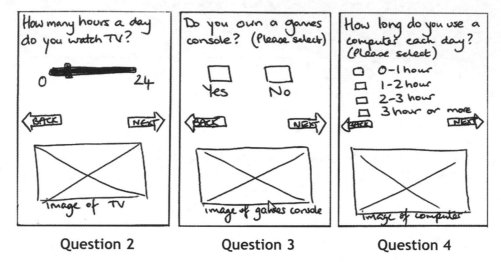

Question 2          Question 3          Question 4

(i) Referring to the designs above, draw a diagram to represent the navigation structure for the carbon footprint calculator.    2

MARKS | DO NOT WRITE IN THIS MARGIN

**19. (a) (continued)**

(ii) At the end of the questions, the user's carbon footprint is calculated.

Explain what is meant by a carbon footprint.    **1**

_____

_____

(iii) When Ally is testing the website, she notices that the total carbon footprint worked out is not calculated correctly.

Explain why this is a logic error and not a syntax error.    **1**

_____

_____

[Turn over

MARKS | DO NOT WRITE IN THIS MARGIN

**19. (continued)**

(b) In the game section of the website, players are shown a board with pairs of picture tiles placed randomly.

These are then flipped over to hide the images. Players have to flip two tiles trying to find two matching images until all pairs have been found.

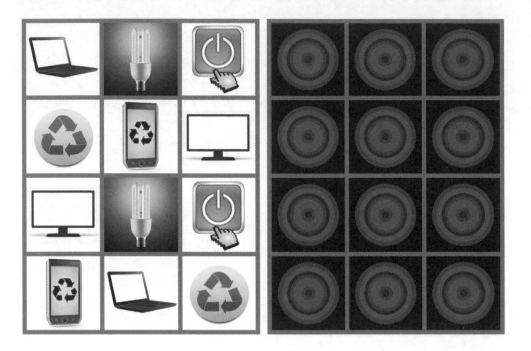

| Images to be paired are displayed to user to be memorised | Tiles are then flipped to start the game |
|---|---|

(i) Identify a situation in the game where Ally will need to implement the following programming constructs.

2

| | |
|---|---|
| **Selection** | |
| **Repetition** | |

MARKS | DO NOT WRITE IN THIS MARGIN

**19. (b) (continued)**

(ii) When a correct pair of images is found, a tip giving advice about energy use or conservation is displayed.

Write the **advice** that should be included with these images.    2

| Image | Advice |
|---|---|
| | "Recycle your old mobile phone to keep hazardous waste out of landfill" |
| | |
| | |

(iii) When creating the website, Ally copies images, sections of text and ideas from a website about energy use.

Explain why she might be in breach of the Copyright Designs and Patents Act.    1

_____

_____

(iv) When the website is released it has a pdf that can be downloaded free.

She has a wireless network available as well as her mobile phone network.

State **one** reason for selecting the wireless option to download the pdf.    1

_____

_____

**Total marks  10**

MARKS

20. A programming language provides the following pre-defined functions.

    move(n)    n = distance moved in pixels

    rotate(d)   d = degrees turned (positive means clockwise)

These can be used by the programmer to draw lines.

A programmer writes the code to draw a square. The code is shown below.

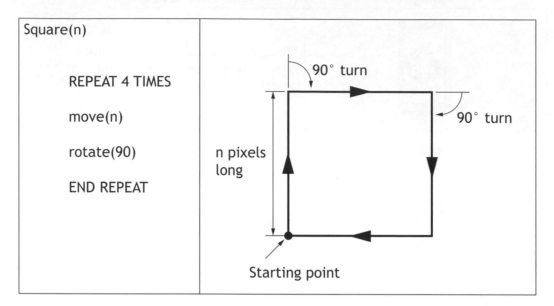

| Square(n) | |
|---|---|
| REPEAT 4 TIMES<br><br>move(n)<br><br>rotate(90)<br><br>END REPEAT | |

(a) Write the code that would draw a hexagon.    3

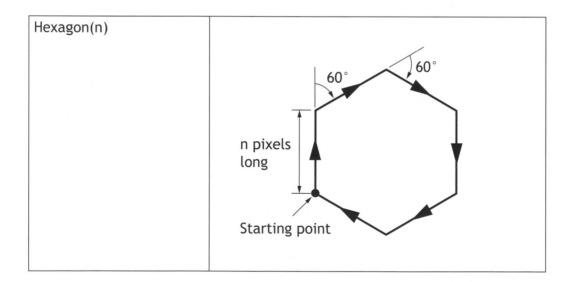

| Hexagon(n) | |
|---|---|
| | |

(b) Describe one way you could make the programmer's code more readable.    1

_____

(c) Suggest a new pre-defined function that could be added to this programming language.    1

_____

MARKS | DO NOT WRITE IN THIS MARGIN

**20. (continued)**

(d)  The following program uses the Square(n) function to draw a pattern.

Two values have been missed out from the code.

Complete the code by filling in the values in the two boxes.    2

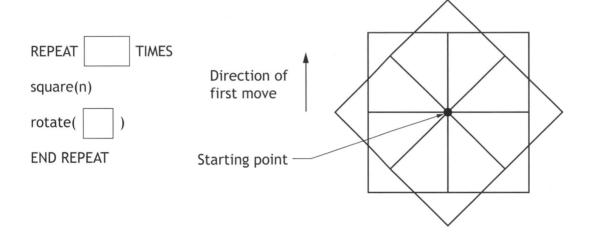

REPEAT ☐ TIMES

square(n)

rotate( ☐ )

END REPEAT

Direction of first move

Starting point

(e)  The shapes that are drawn by the program can be saved as vector graphics.

Describe how a square would be saved as a vector graphic.    2

_____

_____

(f)  Every time a new function is added to the programming language it is designed using pseudocode.

State another design notation that could be used to design the new functions.    1

_____

_____

**Total marks  10**

**[Turn over**

MARKS | DO NOT WRITE IN THIS MARGIN

21. BigTech Gadgets are organising an exhibition to showcase cutting edge developments in technology. BigTech Gadgets want to store the details of products being demonstrated by companies.

Some sample data is shown in the table below.

| Exhibitor Code | Company Name | Area | Stand Number | Product Reference | Item Name | Price (£) |
|---|---|---|---|---|---|---|
| SG100 | FutureTech | Tech Zone | 22 | GD101 | 3D Printer | 1245 |
| SG100 | FutureTech | Tech Zone | 22 | GD102 | 3D Printer XL | 1699 |
| SG176 | Digital80 | Photo Zone | 49 | GD208 | 360 Camera | 800 |
| SG203 | TechATive | Active Zone | 123 | GD187 | GoJet | 1300 |
| SG203 | TechATive | Active Zone | 123 | GD324 | RollerJet | 500 |
| SG489 | ABCMusic | Music Zone | 234 | GD387 | Xkey | 350 |
| SG489 | ABCMusic | Music Zone | 234 | GD367 | Xkey Plus | 500 |
| SG512 | HitechGaming | Games Zone | 288 | GD654 | HowPower2 | 149 |

(a) To avoid data duplication, a database with two linked tables is proposed – EXHIBITOR table and PRODUCT table.

(i) List the fields/attributes that should be included in each table.  2

| EXHIBITOR table | PRODUCT table |
|---|---|
|  |  |

(ii) Identify the foreign key used to link the two tables.  1

_____

(b) When implementing the database, BigTech Gadgets decide to include an image of each product.

Name the field **type** required to store an image.  1

_____

MARKS | DO NOT WRITE IN THIS MARGIN

**21. (continued)**

(c) The Stand Number **must** contain the number of the exhibition stand to be used by the company.

Name the type of validation that should be implemented on this field.    **1**

_____

(d) Visitors to the exhibition will be able to find information using an interactive touchscreen kiosk.

The kiosk includes a map with the location of each zone in the exhibition hall.

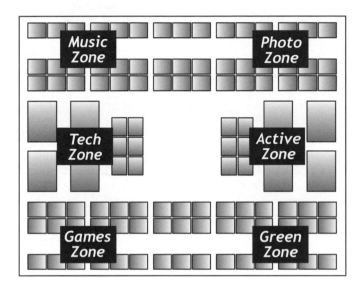

(i) Identify **one** feature that makes this a suitable user interface for a touchscreen kiosk.    **1**

_____

(ii) When the visitor selects the **tech zone button** on the kiosk, a list of companies exhibiting in that area is displayed.

Describe what happens within the database when this button is selected.    **2**

_____

_____

_____

_____

**21. (continued)**

(e) Another screen from the kiosk is shown below.

Identify **two** features used on this screen to aid navigation.

2

_____

_____

**Total marks 10**

**[END OF QUESTION PAPER]**

**MARKS** DO NOT WRITE IN THIS MARGIN

## ADDITIONAL SPACE FOR ANSWERS

**MARKS**  DO NOT WRITE IN THIS MARGIN

**ADDITIONAL SPACE FOR ANSWERS**

[BLANK PAGE]

DO NOT WRITE ON THIS PAGE

[BLANK PAGE]

DO NOT WRITE ON THIS PAGE

**NATIONAL 5**

# 2015

# N5

National
Qualifications
2015

Mark

## X716/75/01

# Computing Science

WEDNESDAY, 6 MAY
9:00 AM – 10:30 AM

**Total marks — 90**

**SECTION 1 — 20 marks**

Attempt ALL questions.

**SECTION 2 — 70 marks**

Attempt ALL questions.

Show all working.

Write your answers clearly in the spaces provided in this booklet. Additional space for answers is provided at the end of this booklet. If you use this space you must clearly identify the question number you are attempting.

Use **blue** or **black** ink.

Before leaving the examination room you must give this booklet to the Invigilator; if you do not, you may lose all the marks for this paper.

SQA

MARKS | DO NOT WRITE IN THIS MARGIN

## SECTION 1 — 20 MARKS

### Attempt ALL Questions

**1.** Convert the decimal number 164 into the equivalent 8-bit binary number. **1**

**2.** A computer program is created to store data about the total number of pupils who pass an exam.

State the most suitable data type for the total. **1**

**3.** The pseudocode shown below uses a simple condition.

IF age < 5 THEN SEND nursery TO DISPLAY

Create a complex condition that will display "school" if a person is between the ages of 5 and 18 inclusive. **2**

MARKS

4.  A web browser keeps a history of websites visited. State **one** other feature of a web browser.

1

_____

_____

5.  This pseudocode allows the user to guess the age of a teddy bear to win it in a competition.

| | |
|---|---|
| Line 1 | RECEIVE guess FROM (INTEGER) KEYBOARD |
| Line 2 | WHILE guess < 1 OR guess > 80 DO |
| Line 3 | SEND "invalid guess: please try again" TO DISPLAY |
| Line 4 | RECEIVE guess FROM (INTEGER) KEYBOARD |
| Line 5 | END WHILE |

Complete the table below to show normal and exceptional test data for guess.

2

| Type of Test Data | Test Data |
|---|---|
| normal | |
| exceptional | |

[Turn over

MARKS | DO NOT WRITE IN THIS MARGIN

6. Kirsty is creating a website for a computer games company. Here is part of the page.

About Us    Contact Details    Online Store    Vacancies

Give **one** reason why the **design** of these links is not good practice.    1

_____

_____

7. Explain the purpose of lines 5 to 8 in this pseudocode.    2

```
        ...
Line 4      SET password TO "h1gh@sch00l"
Line 5      REPEAT
Line 6            SEND "Please enter your password" TO DISPLAY
Line 7            RECEIVE user_guess  FROM (INTEGER) KEYBOARD
Line 8      UNTIL password = user_guess
```

_____

_____

_____

_____

**MARKS**

DO NOT
WRITE IN
THIS
MARGIN

8. Explain why file compression is used before transferring files to cloud storage.

    1

_____

_____

_____

_____

9. Describe **two** methods of improving the readability of code.

    2

Method 1 _____

_____

_____

Method 2 _____

_____

_____

10. State the **data type** of the variable "password" in the code below.

    1

```
...
Line 12    SEND "Please enter your password" TO DISPLAY
Line 13    IF (password < > "h1gh@sch00l") THEN
Line 14        SEND "error: please re-enter password" TO DISPLAY
Line 15    END IF
```

_____

**[Turn over**

MARKS | DO NOT WRITE IN THIS MARGIN

11. Patryk is setting up a network for a school. Give **two** reasons why Patryk would choose a client/server network rather than a peer-to-peer network.    **2**

Reason 1 _____

_____

_____

Reason 2 _____

_____

_____

12. Katie is in her back garden using her smartphone to access her neighbour's wireless network. State the law Katie is breaking.    **1**

_____

13. Describe how **keylogging** can be an online security risk.    **1**

_____

_____

_____

_____

_____

14. A company has both a wired and wireless network. The wireless network allows portability of workstations. Describe **one** advantage for the company of the wired network over the wireless network.    **1**

_____

_____

_____

MARKS | DO NOT WRITE IN THIS MARGIN

**15.** All of the links in this information system have been tested.

## N5 CS Estates

- Houses for Sale
- Houses to Rent
- New Homes
- Contact us

State **one** other type of testing that is used in this information system.　　1

_____

_____

_____

[Turn over

## SECTION 2 — 70 MARKS

### Attempt ALL Questions

16. A retailer wants to set up a website to sell products online.

A template is selected which helps create the website by providing a ready-made structure as shown below.

(a) The template shown above provides consistency of font - colour, style and size of text.

Identify other features to aid good user interface design.

2

_____

_____

_____

_____

MARKS | DO NOT WRITE IN THIS MARGIN

**Question 16 (continued)**

(b) Once the website is created using the template, it is tested using a variety of browsers.

Explain why the webpages appear the same in each web browser.    1

_____

_____

_____

(c) Each web page requires an image of one of the products. A suitable photograph is taken with a digital camera and uploaded to a computer for editing.

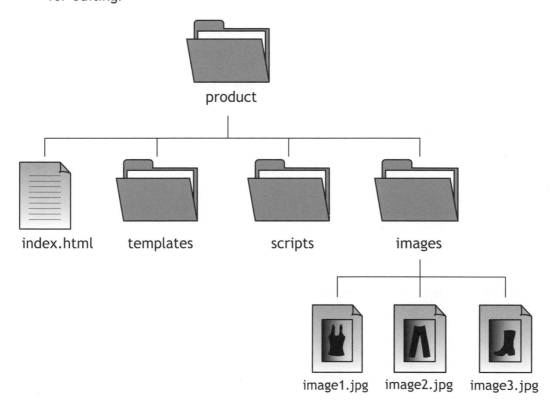

product

index.html    templates    scripts    images

image1.jpg    image2.jpg    image3.jpg

(i) A photograph for the homepage is stored in a folder called **images** as shown above.

The photograph is stored as **image1.jpg**. Name **one** other standard file format for graphics.    1

_____

(ii) State the type of addressing that should be used to include the file **image1.jpg** on the **index.html** page.    1

_____

MARKS | DO NOT WRITE IN THIS MARGIN

**Question 16 (c) (continued)**

(iii) The photograph, before editing, is 4 inch by 6 inch with a resolution of 600 dpi and 24-bit colour depth. Calculate the file size of the photograph.

State your answer using appropriate units. Show all your working.   **3**

(d) A website contains a search engine.

Explain how a search engine is used to produce a list of results.   **2**

_____

_____

_____

_____

_____

_____

**MARKS**

**17.** Pseudocode for a short program is written to calculate VAT on products. Part of the pseudocode is shown below.

> ...
>
> Line 7    SET vatRate TO 0.2
>
> Line 8    RECEIVE productCost FROM (REAL) KEYBOARD
>
> Line 9    SET productVat TO productCost * vatRate

(a) Explain how the value in the variable productCost will be stored in the computer.

2

(b) The program is tested but stops running after a few lines. An error is highlighted.

   (i)  Name the type of translator being used.

1

   (ii) State **one** disadvantage of using this type of translator.

1

(c) When all errors are removed, the completed program is translated. A section of the translated code is shown below.

$$\begin{vmatrix} 1\,0\,1\,1\,0\,0\,0\,1 \\ 0\,0\,1\,0\,1\,1\,1\,0 \\ 1\,1\,1\,1\,0\,1\,0\,1 \\ 0\,1\,1\,0\,1\,1\,1\,0 \end{vmatrix}$$

State the type of programming language the code has been translated into.

1

**[Turn over**

MARKS | DO NOT WRITE IN THIS MARGIN

**Question 17 (continued)**

(d) A diagram of a computer system is shown below.

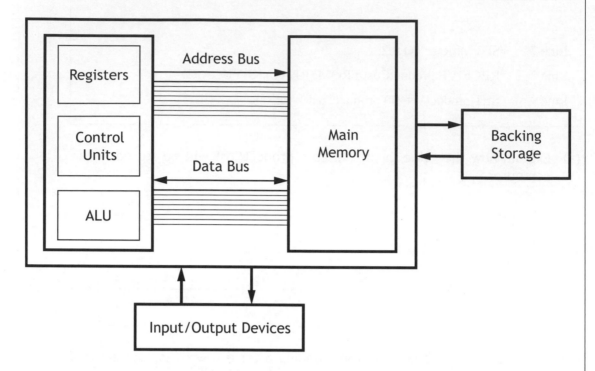

The following part of the program is executed.

```
...

Line 9      SET productVat TO productCost * vatRate
```

Name the part of the computer system that will carry out each of the following tasks during the execution of this line of code.

(i) Carries the location of productCost in main memory.

1

_____

(ii) Transfers the value of productCost from main memory to the processor.

1

_____

(iii) Performs the VAT calculation.

1

_____

MARKS | DO NOT WRITE IN THIS MARGIN

**Question 17 (continued)**

(e) The program is backed-up onto an external hard drive which is connected to the computer using an interface.

Describe **two** purposes of an interface.    2

Purpose 1 _____

_____

Purpose 2 _____

_____

[Turn over

MARKS | DO NOT WRITE IN THIS MARGIN

**18.** Here is the School Learner section of the Scottish Qualifications Authority (SQA) website.

(a) Describe one **purpose** of this section of the website.    1

_____

_____

_____

_____

(b) State the domain name of this webpage URL.    1

_____

(c) This web page design includes several features to aid accessibility.

  (i) Identify **one** of these features.    1

_____

_____

  (ii) Explain how this feature aids accessibility.    1

_____

_____

_____

_____

_____

MARKS | DO NOT WRITE IN THIS MARGIN

**Question 18 (continued)**

(d) The HTML code used to include the SQA logo uses the *img src* tag shown below.

<img src= "../images/sqa-logo.gif">

Name the standard file format used to store the image.     **1**

_____

_____

(e) The web page includes the following navigation feature (breadcrumb).

✕ SQA Home > I am a... > Learner > **School learner**

Explain how this feature aids navigation.     **1**

_____

_____

_____

_____

_____

**[Turn over**

**Question 18 (continued)**

(f) Sally uses the Exam Tools section to search for her own National 5 courses to build her own timetable and print the result.

| List View | Calendar View |
| --- | --- |

| Subject | Qualification | Date | Time | ? |
| --- | --- | --- | --- | --- |
| Italian | National 5 | Thursday 30 April 2015 | 09:00—10:30 | ⊖ |
| Italian | National 5 | Thursday 30 April 2015 | 10:50—11:15 | ⊖ |
| Graphic Communication | National 5 | Thursday 30 April 2015 | 13:00—14:30 | ⊖ |
| Computing Science | National 5 | Wednesday 6 May 2015 | 09:00—10:30 | ⊖ |
| Music | National 5 | Friday 8 May 2015 | 13:00—13:45 | ⊖ |
| English | National 5 | Thursday 14 May 2015 | 09:00—10:00 | ⊖ |
| English | National 5 | Thursday 14 May 2015 | 10:20—11:50 | ⊖ |
| Art and Design | National 5 | Friday 29 May 2015 | 13:30—14:40 | ⊖ |

📇 Export to iCal     🖶 Print     ✉ Email my Timetable

Subject
Graphic Communication  ▼

Qualification
National 5  ▼

Search

Circle **one** example on the webpage above that might make use of Javascript.

1

(g) Describe how the personal National 5 timetable results have been sorted.

2

_____

_____

_____

_____

MARKS | DO NOT WRITE IN THIS MARGIN

**Question 18 (continued)**

(h) Sally downloads a past paper from another area of the website.

Describe **one** concern that Sally might have when she downloads a past paper.

1

_____

_____

_____

_____

[Turn over

**19.** A program is written to calculate the cost of feeding chickens for one month. Chickens eat 5 Kilograms of grain each month. An incomplete design for the program is shown below.

| | |
|---|---|
| Line 1 | SEND "Enter the number of chickens and the cost of grain" TO DISPLAY |
| Line 2 | RECEIVE numberOfChickens FROM (_____) KEYBOARD |
| Line 3 | RECEIVE pricePerKilo FROM (_____) KEYBOARD |
| Line 4 | SEND "Is the grain full price?" TO DISPLAY |
| Line 5 | RECEIVE fullPrice FROM (_____) KEYBOARD |
| Line 6 | IF fullPrice = True THEN |
| Line 7 | SET totalPrice TO numberOfChickens *5*pricePerKilo |
| Line 8 | END IF |
| Line 9 | IF fullPrice = False THEN |
| Line 10 | SET totalPrice TO numberOfChickens *5*(pricePerKilo*0.8) |
| Line 11 | END IF |
| Line 12 | SEND ["The total cost of grain required for" & numberOfChickens & "chickens is £" & totalPrice] TO DISPLAY |

(a) The above design should show the type of data being entered by keyboard in Lines 2, 3 and 5. State the most appropriate data types for the following variables.

3

numberOfChickens _____

pricePerKilo _____

fullPrice _____

MARKS

DO NOT WRITE IN THIS MARGIN

**Question 19 (continued)**

(b)  (i)  State the lines of pseudocode that contain conditional statements.    2

_____

_____

(ii)  State the part of the processor that compares the values in a conditional statement.    1

_____

(c)  The program is later improved to store the totalPrice for each month of a year.

(i)  State the data structure that would be required to store the list of totalPrice values.    2

_____

_____

(ii)  State the **type** of loop required to repeat the code in lines 1 to 12 for each month of the year.  Explain why this type of loop would be used.    2

Type of Loop _____

Explanation _____

_____

_____

[Turn over

MARKS | DO NOT WRITE IN THIS MARGIN

**20.** A supermarket has a flat file database storing information about the 20,000 products it stocks. Part of the database is shown below.

| Dept ID | Dept Name | Department Manager | Product Code | Product Type | Product Name |
|---|---|---|---|---|---|
| 4 | Toiletries | H Green | 100356 | Toothpaste | Dentasparkle |
| 10 | Dry Goods | A Ahmed | 204672 | Cereal | Oatycrunch |
| 6 | Cleaning Products | F McMaster | 318410 | Shoe Polish | Shine |
| 10 | Dry Goods | A Ahmed | 396039 | Packet Soup | Mug-o-Soup |
| 10 | Dry Goods | A Ahmed | 401284 | Biscuits | Choco Snaps |
| 4 | Toiletries | H Green | 672936 | Shower Gel | Clean & Fresh |
| 6 | Cleaning Products | F McMaster | 324221 | Wipes | GermGo |

(a) The design structure of the database looks like this.

| Field Name | Field Type | Field Size | Validation |
|---|---|---|---|
| Dept ID | Number | 2 | >0 and <11 |
| Dept Name | Text | 20 | |
| Department Manager | Text | 20 | |
| Product Code | Text | 6 | Required |
| Product Type | Text | 20 | |
| Product Name | Text | 20 | |

Name **two** types of *validation* that could be applied to the field **Product Code**.

2

Validation 1 _____

Validation 2 _____

(b) The supermarket decides to change the name of the "Cleaning Products" department to "Household Products". Describe a potential problem when changing this data in a *flat file* database design.

1

_____

_____

_____

_____

MARKS | DO NOT WRITE IN THIS MARGIN

**Question 20 (continued)**

(c) A decision is made to modify the design of the database to *linked tables* with two tables: DEPARTMENT and PRODUCT. Each table will have a *primary key*.

    (i) State the purpose of a primary key.      **1**

    _____

    _____

    _____

    (ii) Identify a suitable primary key for each table.      **2**

    DEPARTMENT _____

    PRODUCT     _____

(d) Three new fields

Product In Stock, Product Picture and Product Price

are to be inserted into the PRODUCT table as shown below.

| Product Code | Product Type | Product Name | Product in Stock | Product Picture | Product Price |
|---|---|---|---|---|---|
| 100356 | Toothpaste | Dentasparkle | True | | 1·99 |
| 204672 | Cereal | Oatycrunch | False | | 2·45 |

Name a suitable *field type* for the following new fields.      **2**

Product In Stock _____

Product Picture _____

**[Turn over**

MARKS | DO NOT WRITE IN THIS MARGIN

**Question 20 (continued)**

(e) The supermarket decides to replace its current computers.

Explain **two** ways the company should dispose of the "old" computer systems.

2

[Turn over for Question 21 on *Page twenty-four*

**DO NOT WRITE ON THIS PAGE**

**21.** A program is required to calculate the quantity of bricks required to build a wall. The program will ask the user to enter the dimensions of the wall and a single brick. 1 cm will be added onto the dimensions of the brick to allow for mortar between the bricks. Area of a rectangle is calculated by multiplying the length by height.

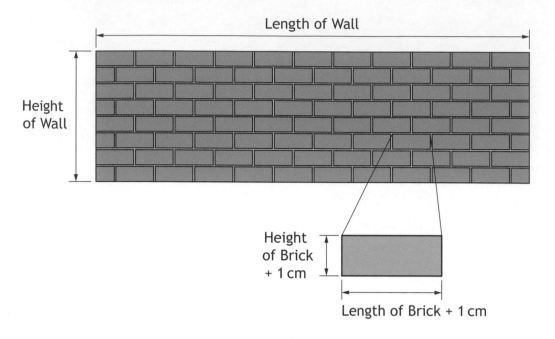

A design for the program is shown below.

| | |
|---|---|
| Line 1 | RECEIVE lengthOfWall FROM (REAL) KEYBOARD |
| Line 2 | RECEIVE heightOfWall FROM (REAL) KEYBOARD |
| Line 3 | RECEIVE lengthOfBrick FROM (REAL) KEYBOARD |
| Line 4 | RECEIVE heightOfBrick FROM (REAL) KEYBOARD |
| Line 5 | SET lengthOfBrick TO lengthOfBrick + 1 |
| Line 6 | SET heightOfBrick TO heightOfBrick + 1 |
| Line 7 | <calculate the quantity of bricks needed> |
| Line 8 | SEND ["The number of bricks needed is –" numberOfBricks] TO DISPLAY |

MARKS | DO NOT WRITE IN THIS MARGIN

**Question 21 (continued)**

(a)  A brick length must be greater than 15 and less than 50.

Using pseudocode or a programming language of your choice, show how input validation could be used to ensure a valid brick length is entered by the user.

3

| Pseudocode [ ] | OR Programming Language [          ] |
| --- |

(b)  Using the information obtained in Lines 1 to 6.

Use pseudocode or a programming language of your choice to show how Line 7 would be implemented.

4

| Pseudocode [ ] | OR Programming Language [          ] |
| --- |

MARKS | DO NOT WRITE IN THIS MARGIN

**Question 21 (continued)**

(c) The program is tested and gives the following output.

The number of bricks needed is: 345.32

The number of bricks needing to be ordered is 346.

Describe how a pre-defined function could be used to ensure that the correct number of bricks is ordered.

2

_____

_____

_____

_____

_____

(d) Mortar is required to hold the bricks in place. The following calculation will be used to calculate the amount of mortar required.

Mortar = (2 * sand) + cement + water

State the number of variables required.

1

_____

MARKS | DO NOT WRITE IN THIS MARGIN

22. Maggie has just started her own photography business taking pictures at weddings and party events. She uses her digital camera with a different 64 Gigabyte memory card for each event.

(a) The memory card in the camera is an example of solid state storage. Explain why this is more suitable for a digital camera than magnetic storage.

2

_____

_____

_____

(b) If a photograph file is 25 Megabytes in size, calculate how many photos Maggie can take at each event before her memory card is full.

Show your working.

2

Maggie transfers the photos to her tablet before the end of each event so that guests can browse the images and then place orders to buy copies.

(c) Describe **two** advantages of using a tablet rather than a laptop computer for this task.

2

Advantage 1 _____

_____

Advantage 2 _____

_____

**MARKS** | DO NOT WRITE IN THIS MARGIN

## Question 22 (continued)

Maggie discovers that using one tablet restricts the number of guests who can view the images during the event and as a result, she does not make many sales.

(d) Maggie decides to use an app called SnapsGalore with cloud storage to organise and manage her photos.

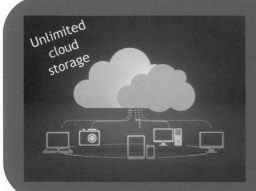

SnapsGalore

Unlimited cloud storage

- No more storage capacity problems
- Unlimited secure storage
- Automatic backup
- Multiple login options
- Cross platform OS compatibility
- Searchable database automatically created when you upload

(i) Describe how cloud storage can be used to provide wider access to the photos.

1

_____

_____

_____

_____

(ii) Identify the feature of the app that allows guests to access the photos even though they have different types of devices.

1

_____

_____

MARKS | DO NOT WRITE IN THIS MARGIN

**Question 22 (continued)**

(e)  Maggie uses the free wireless (WiFi) connection in the venue to transfer the images from the tablet to the SnapsGalore server.

Describe **two** concerns she may have about using the WiFi connection.　　2

Concern 1 _____

_____

_____

Concern 2 _____

_____

_____

**[END OF QUESTION PAPER]**

**ADDITIONAL SPACE FOR ANSWERS**

**MARKS**

**ADDITIONAL SPACE FOR ANSWERS**

*Page thirty-one*

[BLANK PAGE]

DO NOT WRITE ON THIS PAGE

**NATIONAL 5 | ANSWER SECTION**

# SQA AND HODDER GIBSON NATIONAL 5 COMPUTING SCIENCE 2015

## NATIONAL 5 COMPUTING SCIENCE MODEL PAPER 1

### Section 1

1. Binary                                                                    1
2. 33                                                                        1
3. Buses                                                                      1
4. Save them as a standard file format such as RTF                           1
5. Not as expensive and not such a high storage capacity                     2
6. Can be accessed from anywhere in the world                                1
7. Encrypted                                                                  1
8. Copyright, Designs & Patents Act                                          1
9. Pseudocode
   flow chart
   structured diagram                                                        1
10. The first things you type are your user ID and password
    (1 mark) which would then be accessible to the owner of
    the keylogging software (1 mark)                                         2
11. RAM size
    Processor Speed
    Storage capacity
    *One mark for each valid point with a maximum of 2*                      2
12. OR should be an AND                                                       1
13. No meaningful identifiers                                                1
14. Web creation                                                             1
15. Moving to another webpage                                               1
16. Conditional loop                                                        1
17. Syntax error                                                            1

### Section 2

18. (a) Portable
        Smaller footprint                                                    2
    (b) No security
        Difficult to create a methodical backup regime                      2
    (c) Description of:
        • Retina scanning (1 mark)
        • Finger prints (1 mark)                                             2
    (d) Ensure data is wiped from the hard-disc drives
        Physical destruction of hard discs if software cannot
        be used to remove data                                              1
    (e) Ensure that the equipment is recycled or reused
        (1 mark)
        The metals inside should be safely extracted
        (1 mark)                                                            2
19. (a) Height>200 (1 mark) OR (1 mark) weight>2.4 (1 mark)   3
    (b)

| Type of test data | Test Data | |
|---|---|---|
| Normal | Height = 100 | Weight = 2.2 |
| Extreme | Height = 200 | Weight = 2.4 |
| Exceptional | Height = 250 | Weight = 2.5 |

3

(c) As it should be impossible to have a weight or height
    below zero the program should ask for a positive value   1
(d) A wireless connection                                       1

20. (a) REPEAT 4 TIMES
            Forward(100)
            Right(90)
        END REPEAT
        Right(135)
        Move(50)
        Left(135)
        REPEAT 4 TIMES
            Forward(100)
            Right(90)
        END REPEAT                                              3
    (b) • Less memory required
        • Can be re-sized
        • Not resolution dependant
        One mark for each valid point with a maximum of 2.    2
    (c) 400x400x2 = 320000
        320000/8 = 40000 bits
        40000/1024 = 39.0625 Kilobytes                         3
    (d) BMP
        JPEG                                                   1

21. (a) Using small rather than capital letters
        finding the correct letter on the keyboard             2
    (b) RECEIVE answer FROM keyboard (1 mark)
        WHILE answer<>A,B,C or D (1 mark)
            DISPLAY ["Invalid Input, try again"] (1 mark)
            RECEIVE answer FROM keyboard (1 mark)
        END WHILE                                              4
    (c) Initialise the variable wrong and right to the values 0
        (1 mark)
        If the answered received from the keyboard is equal
        to C
        Then add 1 to the correct variable (1 mark)
        If the answer is not equal to C then add 1 to the
        wrong variable (1 mark)                                3
    (d) Shows errors                                           1

22. (a) Line 2 – Value of temperature is 16.3
        Line 3 – Checks if temperature is less than 10 –
        No so goes to line 5
        Line 6 – Checks if temperature is greater than 20 –
        No so goes to line 8
        Line 9 – goes back to line 1 unless switch is off     4
    (b) Mantissa and exponent                                  2
    (c) Boolean                                                1
    (d) Interfaces                                             1
    (e) Internal commentary                                    1

23. (a) Boolean                                                1
    (b) Hyperlink                                              1
    (c) To uniquely identify each record                       1
    (d) Register with the office of the Information
        Commissioner                                          1
    (e) Search on the field New Cd=Yes (1 mark) AND
        (1 mark) field Town="Dundee" (1 mark)                 3

(f) • Data duplication
    • Data inconsistency or update/deletion/insertion anomalies
    • Data integrity errors (due to data inconsistency)
    • Inconsistent search results in multi-value fields
      *Any one for 1 mark*    1

(g) None as an address could be any combination of text    1

24. (a) No return to home page buttons on the webpages    1

   (b) Hyperlinks    1

   (c) Links work
      Checkout works    2

   (d) www.SCOTXCLOTHES.co.uk    2

   (e) Encryption    1

   (f) • Appropriate tags    1
      • Buy a sponsored link    1

   (g) Scripting language    1

25. (a) In case it has been used as a variable previously and already contains a value    1

   (b) Fixed    1

   (c) Arithmetic expression    1

   (d) Total – Integer
      Day – string
      Average – real    3

   (e) One dimensional array    1

# NATIONAL 5 COMPUTING SCIENCE MODEL PAPER 2

## Section 1

1. MP3 has had some data removed while WAV has had no data removed    1

2. Syntax    1

3. Mantissa and exponent    2

4. The bold tag has not been closed    1

5. The address bus    1

6. To store text    1

7. To convert high level language into machine code so that it can be understood by the computer    1

8. Decrease resolution    1

9. (a) Communications Act    1

   (b) Passwords    1

10. No additional hardware or software required.    1

11. Search on the field Town=Inverness (1 mark) AND (1 mark) Date of birth<1/1/1996 (1 mark)    3

12. Alter line 2 from 30 to 31
    Alter line 6 from 30 to 31    2

13. Small children or users with eyesight problems    1

14. Tablet, as it is light and portable and a keyboard isn't necessary    2

## Section 2

15. (a) It takes up less memory
      Can easily re-size objects    2

    (b) SVG    1

    (c) (i) The graphic belongs to someone else – she has broken the Copyright Designs and Patents ACT    1

       (ii) Ask permission from the owner or buy a copy    1

    (d) (i) The file sizes are too large for sending across the Internet    1

       (ii) The quality might not be as good as the original    1

16. (a) UNTIL Pin=4714(1 mark) OR (1 mark) counter=3 (1 mark)    3

    (b) There are two different values for the pin in the program    1

    (c) There are two states to come out of the loop. Either the code is correct or you have had 3 attempts and the code is wrong    2

    (d) You are not sure how many times you are going to go around the loop as you could come out of the loop at the first, second or third attempt    1

    (e) Indentation
       Meaningful identifiers    2

    (f) Integers    1

**17.** (a) SET cost TO 0
RECEIVE weight FROM  keyboard (1 mark)
IF weight<1 THEN
   SET cost TO 5.65(1 mark)
ELSE
    IF weight<2 THEN(1 mark)
      SET cost TO 8.90
    ELSE
      SET cost TO 15.15(1 mark)
    END IF
END IF
SEND["cost of parcel is]cost TO display(1 mark)    **5**

  (b) 0.9, 1.0 ,1.9 ,2.0    **2**

  (c) REPEAT (1 mark)
    RECEIVE weight FROM keyboard (1 mark)
    IF weight<=0 THEN(1 mark)
      SEND[type a valid weight] TO display(1 mark)
    END IF
  UNTIL weight<=0    **4**

**18.** (a) It is a phishing email    **1**

  (b) The fraudsters could use the information to steal your identity, buy goods in your name or access your bank accounts    **1**

  (c)  (i) Doesn't use a standard file format for text    **1**

    (ii) Checks it against known binary patterns of viruses Looks for suspicious activity, such as copying of address books    **2**

  (d) The Computer Misuse Act    **1**

**19.** (a) Internal hyperlink    **1**

  (b) Internal to the website    **1**

  (c) Relative referencing    **1**

  (d) Reduce the sample rate    **1**

  (e) Search engine works, navigation bars go to correct pages, shopping cart works    **2**

  (f) Same type of navigation bar that appears on his homepage, the three red hyperlinked boxes    **1**

  (g) Layout on each screen/screen design, method of interaction, choice of font/size/styles, accessible to all users    **2**

  (h) Javascript    **1**

**20.** (a) 'Gender' field into ascending order and 'surname' (or class code) field into ascending order    **2**

  (b)  (i) Student no    **1**

    (ii) Foreign key is an attribute which appears in another table as a primary key    **1**

  (c) Text    **1**

  (d) Student no, date of birth and class code    **2**

  (e) Restricted choice    **1**

  (f) Alice Burns and Jasmine Dunsmuir    **1**

  (g) • Searching/sorting can be done very quickly/more easily
    • Data can be updated very quickly/more easily
    • Data analysis and reporting can be done very easily
    • Searches and sorts are done accurately
    • Easier to backup
    • Less space taken up    **2**

**21.** (a) Along the data bus    **1**

  (b) Faster performance with memory intensive applications such as video editing    **1**

  (c) USB – attaching external Flash drives Firewire – attaching digital video cameras    **2**

  (d) Advantage – difficult to damage Disadvantage – more expensive per gigabyte, not available in the all capacities    **2**

  (e) Touchscreen, multi-touch (pinching)    **2**

**22.** (a) One dimensional integer array    **2**

  (b) Real    **1**

  (c) Fixed loop    **1**

  (d) A negative number, text    **2**

  (e) Input validation    **1**

# NATIONAL 5 COMPUTING SCIENCE MODEL PAPER 3

## Section 1

1. • Adjust your chair and desk so that you are sitting without straining
   • Use alternative mice or keyboards
   • Take regular breaks
   • Use speech recognition software    1

2. Can be opened by any type of computer system without the need for specific applications or operating system software    1

3. Indentation (1 mark)
   Meaningful variable names (1 mark)    2

4. Advantage – Higher resolution therefore better quality images (1 mark)
   Disadvantage – Takes up much more memory than previously so will store less images on her SSD card (1 mark)    2

5. Pre-defined (1 mark) functions (1 mark)    2

6. The Data Transfer rate of USB3 is much faster than USB2    1

7. • Home working decreases the amount of car travel
   • Video conferencing reduces the amount of flights taken by business people    1

8. (a) A pre-defined function eg INT or Round    1
   (b) Real    1

9. ROM is permanent. RAM and Registers are temporary and lose all the data when there is no power    1

10. • Validate data that is entered into forms
    • Give warnings and confirmation messages to users
    • Add check buttons, radio buttons and command buttons
    • Provide information on the system date and time
    *Any two from the above list*    2

11. When you saw that there was a great deal of data being duplicated    1

12. He was committing a crime through the Communications Act by accessing someone else wi-fi without permission (1 mark)
    Wi-fi has less bandwidth than wired access and so is slower to access data (1 mark)    2

13. Structure – one dimensional array (1 mark)
    Data Type – integer (1 mark)    2

## Section 2

14. (a)

| Field Name | Field size | Field Type |
|---|---|---|
| Forename | 25 | *Text* |
| Surname | 25 | *Text* |
| Address | 25 | *Text* |
| Town | 25 | *Text* |
| Type of Credit card | | |
|    Visa | 1 | *Boolean* |
|    Mastercard | 1 | *Boolean* |
|    Amex | 1 | *Boolean* |
| Credit Card Number | 16 | *Numeric* |
| Expiry Date | 8 | *Date* |
| Card Security Code | 3 | *Numeric* |

   2

  (b) All the fields require a presence check except only one required in type of credit card    2

  (c) Credit card no, expiry date, card security code    2

  (d) Credit card number    1

15. (a) IF letter="M" (1 mark) AND (1 mark) x<100 THEN (1 mark)
    SET x=x+1 (1 mark)    4

  (b) Nothing happens    1

  (c) String    1

  (d) SET score TO (1 mark) score +10 (1 mark)    2

  (e) Amount of RAM    1

16. (a) Berlin    1

  (b) Doesn't take into account if two teams have the same highest score    1

  (c) A typing error eg ENF IF    1

  (d) one dimensional string array    2

  (e) Change variable highest to lowest (1 mark)
    change < to > (1 mark)
    change "the winning team" to the "losing team" (1 mark)    3

  (f) Add four more team names to line 1
    Add four more points to line 2
    Change 4 to 8 in line 4    3

17. (a) GroundNews.org.uk    1

  (b) Home page    1

  (c) You are taken to a page on Africa on the site    1

  (d) It's only related to this website    1

  (e) MPEG4    1

  (f) Limited controls
    Straight forward navigation
    Good visual layout    2

  (g) Limited RAM
    Limited processing speed    2

  (h) Ensure that the stories aren't copied from other news channels    1

(i) • Hyperlinks take them to the correct pages
   • Search works
   • Video works     3

18. (a) Line 1  RECEIVE age FROM keyboard (1 mark)
    Line 2  IF age<18 THEN (1 mark)
    Line 3    SEND["Your ticket cost £ 5"] TO DISPLAY
    Line 4  ELSE
    Line 5    IF age<27 THEN (1 mark)
    Line 6      SEND["Your ticket cost £ 10"] TO DISPLAY
    Line 7    ELSE  (1 mark)
    Line 8      SEND["Your ticket cost £ 20"] TO DISPLAY
    Line 9    END IF
    Line 10  END IF     4

(b) Integer     1

(c) 17, 18, 26, 27     2

(d) Easier to spot errors during execution     1

(e) • Will run faster than interpreted version
   • Doesn't need translator     2

(f) The compiled version is in machine code     1

19. (a) Capacity and data transfer speed     2

(b) Compress to MP3     1

(c) Could access the files from anywhere in the world     1

(d) Passwords, encryption     2

(e) (i) Bit-mapped pixel by pixel     2
    (ii) 1200 x 1200 x 2 = 2880000 bits (1 mark)
      2880000 / 8 = 360000 bytes  (1 mark)
      360000 / 1024 = 351.6 Kb  (1 mark)     3

20. (a) Flight number then surname     2

(b) Duplication of data     1

(c) Denial of Service Attack     1

(d) Simple short commands such as Run, Insert etc (1 mark)
Restricted choices from pop-up menus, check boxes and radio buttons (1 mark)     2

(e) • Peripherals run at different speeds from the processor
   • Some peripherals are analogue and the signals need to be converted to digital     2

# NATIONAL 5 COMPUTING SCIENCE 2014

## Section 1

1. *Explain:*
An internal hyperlink points to a file/another page within a website
An external hyperlink points to another website

2. *Name:* Browser

3. *Calculate:*
400 × 600 × 8 =1920000 (bits)

1920000/8 = 240000 (bytes)
240000 (bytes)/1024
= 234.375 (Kb)

4. *Name:* Arithmetic Logic Unit/ALU

5. *Convert:* 00101111

6. *State any one from:*
   • Data duplication
   • Data inconsistency or update/deletion/insertion anomalies
   • Data integrity errors (due to data inconsistency)
   • Inconsistent search results in multi-value fields

7. *Identify any one from:*
   • Encryption
   • Password/PIN
   • Biometric

8. *State any one from:*
   • Reduces the chance of human error
   • Does not require the user to type a text response
   • Speeds up the ordering process as inputs are reduced to mouse clicks
   • Allows the use of a touchscreen
   • Do not have to remember any types of pizza on offer

9. *Describe:*
   • Check navigation
   • Check all hyperlinks/hotspots
   • Ensure graphics are not pixelated
   • Ensure audio clips run
   • Any JavaScript issues
   • Check compatibility with browsers

10. *State any one from:*
    • Can access data from any computer device remotely
    • No requirement for own servers
    • Less need for own technical support on site
    • Automatic backup/recovery of data

11. *State any one from each list:*
    Client Server
    • Data can be stored/accessed centrally
    • Only accessible by registered users
    • Different access rights for users
    • Shared peripherals
    • Expensive with explanation

    Peer to Peer
    • Resources stored on device available to other peers
    • No centralised stored
    • Not as secure as Client Server
    • Risk from viruses

12. *Explain:*
    Line 2: Value stored in variable level (12) is outwith range, so loop implemented
    Line 3: Message sent to display
    Line 4: New value entered

**13.** An example of:
- Non numeric
- Out of range
- Real numbers

**14.** (a) Line 3

(b) Replace OR with AND

## Section 2

**15.** (a) *State:*
http://www.holibobs.co.uk/greece/crete234.html

(b) *State:*

(i) Tags
Styles

(ii) *Explain:*
External link to another site/server

(iii) Any acceptable use of Javascript to create interactivity or dynamic content on this webpage

(c) • mp4 – 'Download Videos' or 'Virtual Tour of Property' buttons
• jpeg – Any example of a graphic on page or 'Photo Gallery' or 'Location Map' or 'Villa picture' or 'Holibobs Icon' or 'Weather Widget'

(d) *Explain:*
- Reduced colour depth
- Smaller file size
- Allows image to load faster

(e) • Price descending
• Resort ascending

**16.** (a) *State:*
6

(b) *Candidate answer must include:*
4 values input – Water Cost, Flavour Cost, Labour Cost, Selling Price

Manufacturing Cost = Water Cost + Flavouring Cost + Labour

Profit = Selling Price – Manufacturing Cost

Output of Profit

(c) (i) *State:*
(Input) Validation

(ii)

| Test Data (Flavouring) | Type of Test Data |
|---|---|
| 0.05 | exceptional |
| 0.45 | normal |
| 0.10 | extreme |
| 0.50 | extreme |

**17.** (a) *Answers should identify parts of **this** webpage which will not be suitable on a small screen device.*
*For example:*
- Navigation bar does not fit across small screen
- Too many columns
- Too much information for small screen
- Icons too small to click on right hand side
- Would take too long to load images on portable device

(b) *Explain:*
Personal details transmitted in code cannot be read (by hackers)
**OR**
Keeps personal data secure/safe
**OR**
Only the company can access the encrypted data

(c) *Explain:*
Different operating systems on devices
**OR**
Hardware differences (resolution, dual core processor, memory etc)

(d) *Identify any two from:*
- Touchscreen
- Microphone
- Camera

(e) *Complete the table:*
Smartphone
Storage: Solid state
Reason: Low power/size/robust/ transfer rate

Web Server
Storage: Magnetic
Reason: Large capacity/low cost per Mb

DVD
Storage: Optical
Reason: Portable/read by range of devices

(f) Random Access Memory

**18.** (a) (i) Line 17

(ii) Line 20

(iii) Line 16

(b) *State:* Syntax

(c) (i) *State:* Conditional (loop)

(ii) *State:* Real number >20 and <70

(d) *State:*
Structure Chart
Structure Diagram
Flow Chart

(e) *State:* Interpreter

*Explain:* No need to leave the programming environment/tracing facilities/debugging facilities

(f) Interface

**19.** (a) (i) 1 mark for showing a linear design
1 mark for all arrows

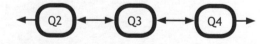

(ii) *Explain:* Carbon Footprint is the overall harmful emissions associated with a life of a product/time frame

(iii) *Explain:* Logic error executes but gives wrong answer

Calculation incorrectly implemented

(b) (i) *Identify:*

Selection:  user clicks on tile
Repetition:  repeat turn/repeat tile turning until tiles matched/repeat game

(ii) *Candidate should specify energy saving tip relating to image.*
*For example:*

Diagram 1:
Switch off device when not in use to save energy.
Don't leave devices on standby when not in use.

Diagram 2:
Laptops use less power.
Switch laptop to hibernate when not in use.
Reduce brightness to save power.
Dispose of laptops correctly

(iii) *Explain:*
Demonstrate understanding of copying work created by others.
For example:
• Use of images without copyright permission
• Plagiarism of other persons writing

(iv) *State:*
Faster transfer/download speed
Downloading via mobile might use up data (allowance)

20. (a) *Code:*
```
REPEAT 6
move(n)
rotate(60)
END REPEAT
```

(b) *Describe any one from:*
• Internal commentary
• Meaningful identifiers
• Modularisation
• White space
• Indentation

(c) *Any suitable function. Apply knowledge to the scenario.*
*For example:*
• Polygon (any shape)
• Text tool
• Fill

(d) 8
45

(e) Square required complete attributes, eg:
startx, starty
length, rotation, line fill

(f) *State:*
Structure Chart or
Flow Diagram/Chart

21. (a) (i) *Identify:*

| EXHIBITOR table | PRODUCT table |
|---|---|
| exhibitor code<br>company name<br>area<br>stand number | exhibitor code<br>product ref<br>item name<br>price |

(ii) *Identify:* Exhibitor code

(b) *Name:*
Object
Graphic
Container

(c) *Name:* Presence check

(d) (i) *Identify from diagram:*
• Large areas to make selection easy
• Large readable text
• Uncluttered screen

(ii) • Macro/Script/search program activated
• Search carried out using
Area field = Tech Zone

(e) *Identify any two from:*
• Breadcrumb
• Highlighted selection
• Back/Forward buttons
• Search (bar)
• Home (button)

# NATIONAL 5 COMPUTING SCIENCE 2015

## Section 1

1. 1 0 1 0 0 1 0 0

2. Integer

3. (age >= 5) AND (age <=18)
   2 conditions correct − 1 mark
   AND − 1 mark

4. Shortcuts/favourites/bookmarks/ refresh/stop button/home button/search box/address bar/tabbed browsing

   Change user settings (font size etc.)
   Change default homepage
   Customising toolbars

5. Normal
      >=1 and <=80 (1 mark)
   Exceptional
      <1 or >80 (1 mark)
   Any example of text

6. Suitable reason why the links are inconsistent

7. The user will be required to enter a password (1 mark)
   Until the correct password is entered (1 mark)

8. *Any one valid:*
   • Upload/transfer faster
   • More files can be stored

9. *Any two of:*
   • Emphasise keywords
   • Internal commentary
   • Indentation
   • White space
   • Meaningful identifiers
   • Modular code
   • Use of parameter passing

10. String

11. Easier to backup files (1)
    Easier to implement different levels of access (security) (1)
    Centralised storage (1)
    Users have usernames and passwords (1)

12. Communications (Act)

13. Description of sensitive information (PIN, passwords etc) being logged.

14. *Any one valid answer for wired:*
    • It's more secure/security
    • It's more reliable/reliability
    • Upload/download speed faster

15. • Matches user interface (correct layout)
    • Spelling/Grammar
    • Graphic quality
    • Colour scheme useable
    • Graphics load correctly
    • Works on multiple browsers

## Section 2

16. (a) *Any two suitable features relating to user interface:*
    • Interactive elements such as buttons all same shape, size, colour
    • Appropriate navigation
    • Consistent/appropriate layout of elements
    • Consistent colour theme
    • Accessibility Options

(b) The web page code/HTML/CSS determines the appearance of the web page not the browser

(c) (i) *Answer should name any standard file format for graphics:*
   • gif
   • bmp
   • png

   (ii) Relative

   (iii) 4 × 6 × 600 × 600 (1 mark)
        × 24 bits (1 mark)
        (207360000 bits/8/1024/1024)
        = 24.72 Mb (1 mark)

(d) *A description that includes:*
    • matching keywords/search criteria entered by user
    • database of known pages/stored metadata

17. (a) Mantissa and exponent

   (b) (i) Interpreter

      (ii) *Any one for 1 mark:*
         • Additional RAM required
         • Increased processing required
         • (Could run more slowly)
         • Loops translated multiple times

   (c) Machine Code or Binary

   (d) (i) Address Bus

      (ii) Data Bus

      (iii) Arithmetic Logic Unit (ALU)

   (e) *Any two for 1 mark each:*
      • Temporary storage of data
      • Handling of status signals
      • Data conversion − serial to parallel
      • Voltage conversion
      • Communication between two devices

18. (a) *Answer identifies one aim of school learner section of SQA site:*
      • provide information about exams
      • provide resources to help study for exams

   (b) Domain name of URL:
      (www.)sqa.org.uk

   (c) (i) *Any one from the following:*
         • Listen to the page option
         • Text resize option
         • Change colour scheme/Alter background colour
         • Read transcript of video

      (ii) • Screen reader reads out text of page and graphic captions to help those with sight problems or reading difficulty to access page content.
          • Text resize option can be used by those with visual impairment to enlarge text making it easier to see and read.
          • Changing colour scheme allows people with dyslexia or colour blindness or vision problems to access content.
          • Altering colour combinations makes text easier to distinguish.
          • Transcript of video makes video content accessible to those with hearing impairment.

   (d) Gif

(e) • Helps user view path taken to reach this page
   • Useful to retrace steps and go back to previous pages
   • Useful in indicating section of current page to orientate user

(f)

(g) *Complex sort described:*
   • Date ascending
   • Time ascending

(h) • Containing a virus
   • May not have correct software
   • File may be too large

**19.** (a) • Line 2 — Integer
   • Line 3 — Real
   • Line 5 — Boolean

(b) (i) • Line 6
       • Line 9

   (ii) Arithmetic Logic Unit (ALU)

(c) (i) An array (1 mark)
       Of Reals (1 mark)

   (ii) Unconditional/fixed loop (1 mark)
       The program loops a known (12) number of times. (1 mark)

**20.** (a) Presence check
   Length check/field length

(b) *Potential for increased errors due to:*
   • Update anomalies
   • Lots of changes being made

(c) (i) Unique identifier for a row/record in a table.

   (ii) Dept ID
       Product Code

(d) Boolean
   Graphic/Object/Container

(e) *1 mark for each bullet (max 2):*
   • Removing data from hard drive
   • Using collection company
   • Recycle individual components appropriately
   • Dispose of dangerous elements

**21.** (a) *1 mark each for:*
   • Conditional loop
   • Input of brick length from user
   • Correct complex conditions attached to loop (>15 AND <50)

(b) *1 mark each for:*
   • Assignment
     any relevant example
   • Calculating wall area
     lengthOfWall * heightOfWall
   • Calculating brick area
     lengthOfBrick * heightOfBrick
   • Dividing wall area by brick area

(c) A function could be used to remove the decimal places from the number (1 mark) and then 1 could be added on (1 mark).
   **or**
   int(numberOFBricks) + 1

   Marks allocated as:
   int(numberOFBricks) (1 mark)
   +1 (1 mark)

(d) 4

**22.** (a) *Any two from:*
   • Solid state has no moving parts
   • Camera is portable, size/weight of storage should be considered
   • Robust storage more suitable
   • Solid state can be removed
   • Transfer/storage of data faster to/from solid state

(b) Total storage (1 mark)
   64Gb = 64 × 1024 = 65,536 (Mb)

   Number of photos (1 mark)
   65,536/25 = 2,621.44
   rounded down to 2621 photos

(c) *Any two advantages of tablet PC over laptop relevant to scenario:*
   • Simple interface for range of users/guests
   • Touch screen easy to use for guests
   • More portability to pass round at event/lightweight
   • More robust when being passed around

(d) (i) *Use of cloud:*
       • Remote access from any location with internet connection
       • Centrally accessible storage location
       • Provide login to guests who can access the files on their own device

   (ii) Cross platform OS compatibility — runs on variety of operating systems

(e) *Concerns about Wifi:*
   • Slow data transfer speed compared to wired connection
   • Security issues
   • Limited range/lack of coverage/loss of connection in parts of venue
   • Signal interference from other devices

# Acknowledgements

Permission has been sought from all relevant copyright holders and Hodder Gibson is grateful for the use of the following:

Image © slava296/Shutterstock.com (2014 page 8);
Image © Perfect Vectors/Shutterstock.com (2014 page 8);
Image © A-R-T/Shutterstock.com (2014 page 22);
Image © Kostsov/Shutterstock.com (2014 page 22);
Image © wwwebmeister/Shutterstock.com (2014 page 22);
Image © Nicholas 852/Shutterstock.com (2014 page 22);
Image © Pavel Ignatov/Shutterstock.com (2014 page 22);
Image © Duna Csongor/Shutterstock.com (2014 page 22);
Image © Pavel Ignatov/Shutterstock.com (2014 page 23);
Image © wwwebmeister/Shutterstock.com (2014 page 23);
Image © A-R-T/Shutterstock.com (2014 page 23);
Image © Hubis/Shutterstock.com (2015 page 8);
Image © Rashevskyi Viacheslav/Shutterstock.com (2015 page 21);
Image © Matthew Cole/Shutterstock.com (2015 page 21);
Image © musicman/Shutterstock.com (2015 page 28).

Hodder Gibson would like to thank SQA for use of any past exam questions that may have been used in model papers, whether amended or in original form.